Plant Spirit Wisdom

Plant Spirit Wisdom

Connect with your Plant Allies
for powerful healing
and guidance

Karine Gordineer

CICO BOOKS

Published in 2026 by CICO Books
An imprint of Ryland Peters & Small Ltd
20–21 Jockey's Fields
London WC1R 4BW
1452 Davis Bugg Road
Warrenton, NC 27589
www.rylandpeters.com
Email: euregulations@rylandpeters.com

10 9 8 7 6 5 4 3 2 1

A CIP record for this book is available from the British Library.
US Library of Congress CIP data has been applied for.

ISBN: 978-1-80065-579-9

Printed in China

Illustrator: Carolina Zambrano
Commissioning editor: Kristine Pidkameny
Desk editor: Imogen Valler-Miles
Senior designer: Emily Breen
Art director: Sally Powell
Creative director: Leslie Harrington
Head of production: Patricia Harrington
Publishing manager: Carmel Edmonds

The authorised representative in the EEA is
Authorised Rep Compliance Ltd.,
Ground Floor. 71 Lower Baggot Street,
Dublin, D01 P593, Ireland
www.arccompliance.com

MIX
Paper | Supporting responsible forestry
FSC® C008047

SAFETY NOTES

Some plants are poisonous—they can cause severe allergic reactions and potentially be fatal. Do not touch or ingest any part of a plant or its remedies (including teas, oils, and essences) unless you are absolutely sure it is safe to do so, and keep them away from pets and children.

It is the sole responsibility of the reader to correctly identify a plant before working with it. Seek advice from a qualified professional if unsure. Neither the author nor the publisher can be held responsible for any claim arising out of the general information, recipes, practices, and suggestions provided in this book.

While the use of plants, herbs, essential oils, and other remedies may refer to healing benefits, they are not intended to replace diagnosis of illness or ailments, or healing or medicine. Always consult your doctor or other health professional in the case of illness.

Essential oils are very powerful and potentially toxic if used too liberally. Please follow the advice given on the label and never use the oils neat on bare skin, or if pregnant. If you are pregnant, have a medical condition, or are on medication, seek professional advice before using essential oils. The safe and proper use of candles, incense, matches, lighters, and smudge sticks is the sole responsibility of the person using them. Do not leave a burning flame unattended. Never burn a flame on or near anything that might catch fire. Keep fire out of the reach of children and pets.

Contents

Introduction: The Journey Begins

It is my greatest joy to invite you, dear reader, on a journey to explore the world of plant sentience and communication. Take a walk with me into Earth's geological history as we journey through the earliest beginnings of "Earth time," exploring the interval before plants even existed. Discover the remarkable resilience of plants through the eons and the lessons they have imparted to humanity, which remind us of the importance of honoring and reconnecting with the green beings.

You will learn about plant consciousness as more than just a concept; you'll experience it firsthand as you are guided through the ways in which plants speak to us before learning how to communicate with them through the shamanic journey, ceremony, meditation, and other activities. These practices are designed to facilitate and strengthen your sacred relationships with the plants. As you develop skills of awareness and deep listening, the plants' voices will come alive in ways you've never experienced before.

This explorative journey introduces you to the Plant Ally relationship and uncovers how these botanical bonds can aid in healing, foster emotional wellness and balance,

and nourish this rooted kinship. You will meet specific Plant Allies who wish to share their individual messages, encouraging you to look beyond physical reality into the souls of the plants and nature.

I use the terms Plant Spirits and Plant Allies throughout the book. A Plant Spirit refers to the essence of a plant beyond its physical presence. In Plant Spirit work, you may find this term used interchangeably with "plant being." The term Plant Ally refers to a specific plant we have a special bond with. These are plants we will turn to repeatedly for their wisdom and healing frequencies.

Throughout the book, I provide a common name and the scientific name (presented in italic type) when I refer to specific plants. A single plant may have many common names but it will only have one scientific name, made up of two parts: genus and species. The genus identifies a group of plants that share key characteristics; the species distinguishes the individual plant within that genus. Often, a single genus will contain many different species.

It is my deepest desire that the wisdom imparted herein will encourage a return to the sacred relationship with Earth and all Her beings, which we all once shared.

CHAPTER 1

THE POWER OF PLANTS

Often overlooked as mere background greenery, plants are extraordinary beings, essential to life. In the pages ahead, you'll glimpse their rich history and discover what makes them remarkable—not only as unique species but as catalysts of transformation, bridging ancient tradition and modern science. As you are introduced to plant consciousness, you will begin to learn to listen and to connect.

Conscious Beings

All beings on Earth have consciousness. This concept was, and is, a fundamental truth for many, if not all, cultures that continue to live close to the natural world and its rhythms. It is a tenet our ancient ancestors believed in deeply, reflected throughout their lives, actions, and attitudes. As an integral and special part of nature, it was understood that all plants are conscious beings with immense wisdom and healing powers extending beyond the traditional herbal remedies that work primarily on the physical body. Our ancestors knew that the Spirits of the Plants could be called upon to aid in healing the human soul or spirit, transporting the seeker into unseen realms, with the plant beings acting as guides and intermediaries within the spirit world.

Within this realm, the querent could receive answers to many questions—even those questions with seemingly unknowable answers—experience healing ceremonies, psychically travel great distances, understand and predict weather patterns, locate food sources, and even learn the healing properties of the plants themselves and the specific ways to extract them. The individuals who "walked between the worlds" in this way brought back sacred knowledge to benefit not only themselves but their village as a whole. This knowledge was honored and respected, forming bonds between the people, the Earth, and the beings of nature that lasted for generations. But as humanity has stepped farther away from this ancient trust, we have caused harm both to the Earth and to one another.

Although the crises we face today are vast and layered, rooted in histories of injustice, inequality, and displacement, a significant thread that runs through them is our separation from nature. Living as though we are apart from the very forces that give us life has created a deep rift within our spirits. This disconnection has manifested as an

unspoken grief and unease echoing outward into global discord, ecological collapse, emotional and mental distress, and physical disease. As we step back into "right relationship" with the Earth and all Her beings, we begin to repair this rift within ourselves, reflecting this much-needed light and healing back out into our world.

The Spirits of the Plants are unique and willing partners in this process. They act as conduits, companions, and midwives of remembrance, guiding us gently back into the sacred rhythms of the everyday and into a deeper kinship with all life.

Reconnecting

Within all of us exists the knowledge of interspecies communication—not only the knowledge but also the memory of this ability. We all have places along our familial or spiritual lineages that echo the experience of exchanging information and living peacefully with all life-forms on the planet. Like a distant daydream, a part of us remembers communicating with and learning from the stars, the Sun, the Moon, the animals, and the plants, too! And this part of us longs to return to these ways.

Many Indigenous cultures believe that the Plant Spirits are our ancestors; that they are here to nurture and guide us. Plants do an incredible job of caring for us because they provide us with food, medicines, clothing, our homes, and even the air we breathe. When we learn to become aware of, sense, and decipher their language, we find that the line of communication is very much alive as the plants become trusted allies, mentors, and friends, offering up comfort, wisdom, and connection wherever and whenever we need it most.

Early humans relied on their spiritual and energetic partnerships with plants and other beings to gain knowledge, unlocking the mysteries of the natural world and the invisible realms that taught them how to provide food, shelter, and clothing, craft healing medicines, channel artistic expression, and create ceremony. Steeped within all cultures around the globe is local native wisdom and lore of the spirits of nature in their various forms. Although the Plant Spirits were not the only spiritual connection our ancestors relied on, they were a significant and universal one common to various cultures around the world. Their universality is what makes them unique in bridging the current divide in human consciousness with the natural world, our Mother Earth.

This is a language that belongs to all of us and one that we can all relearn; a connection that needs to be reawakened and strengthened. In doing so, we help to restore the balance so needed on this planet and, in the process, create a shared home of beauty, wonder, peace, and fulfillment.

PRACTICE

Discover the Plants Growing Around You

In this exercise, you'll begin the process of rediscovering the plants that cohabit the area where you live or frequent. It will only take 5–10 minutes and can be done in your yard, in the street right outside your door, or at a local park. Artistic acumen is not needed—all you'll need is a simple phone camera or a drawing pad and pencil.

1 Venture outdoors to your chosen location and take photos of one to three plants. Alternatively, create a few quick sketches.

2 Make a note of the characteristics of the plants, including their height, color, stem type (for example, whether it is smooth or hairy), leaf shapes, and flower color and type.

3 If you don't know the names of the plants, use books or reliable sources on the internet to learn their names, then research the plants to learn a little bit more about them, including their growing patterns and local lore.

A History of Resilience

This gentle, temperate Earth we've come to know, love, and rely on was not always the way it is today. In fact, if we could travel back through Earth's history a few billion years, our planet in its infancy would be unrecognizable to us. Born from a dervish of dust particles and gases cast off from the formation of our Sun and solar system, the early phases of our planet's life were chaos personified. The air was toxic and unbreathable. The ground, fluid and molten, was continually in motion, a veritable "magma ocean." The cataclysmic temperament of this period garnered itself the name of the Hadean Eon after Hades, the Greek god of the underworld.

Over the next one billion years, the Earth cooled sufficiently enough for water vapor in the atmosphere to condense, creating clouds that saturated the Earth in life-giving rain. Panthalassa was the first mega-ocean, a liquid nursery to all the life-forms that would ever push forth from this universal mother.

The earliest ancestors of modern-day plants were formed some 2.4 to 2.7 billion years ago. Cyanobacteria, the first known life-forms on Earth, were one of the most significant creations to emerge, and were the first organisms to perform oxygenic photosynthesis. This was a major turning point in Earth's evolution because these early plant ancestors did not just *adapt* to this highly unstable environment, they *changed* the environment, evolving the atmosphere from one of a suffocating toxic sauna into one that would support all life as we know it.

Throughout the subsequent passing of the eons, plants experienced and bore witness to seismic shifts in the land masses, massive floods, droughts, flourishing evolutions of creatures, and mass extinctions, some of which nearly destroyed all life on the planet. And through it all, plants continued to be silent witnesses, sentinels, developing adaptations that would first allow them to leave the water, then move away from the water. Finally, advancing their methods of reproduction guaranteed their continued success. They learned how to work and cooperate with other species, coevolving with other plants, insects and other animals, and microorganisms.

This high-level timeline and these evolutionary milestones, framed against the incredible length of time that plants have been successfully thriving on the planet, magnificently illustrate their adaptability and resilience; just two of the lessons plants have to impart to humanity.

Lessons for Humanity

Through careful observation of nature, we can learn from the non-human beings on the planet, especially from the plants. Plants are masters at not only surviving but thriving and adapting in all types of environments and during cataclysmic events.

The term "biomimicry" was first developed in 1997 and popularized by the author Janine M. Benyus in her book of the same name. Biomimicry is the practice of watching and mimicking nature to find sustainable answers to problems faced by humans. Although the term is new, humanity has been learning from nature and plants for millennia.

- In Indigenous, desert-dwelling cultures in areas such as North Africa and the Middle East, people observed how succulents stored water in their thick, waxy tissues. They saw how efficient and effective this was and created their own water storage containers using gourds and clay vessels. These same principles were used to design their homes to stay cool.
- Many vining plants, such as Wild Grape (*Vitis vinifera*), which naturally spiral, twist, and cling to trees using helical growth and tendrils (appendages of climbing plants, often growing in spiral patterns), inspired early humans to weave natural ropes for carrying tools, constructing shelters, and binding items. In tropical regions, Rattan (*Calamus* species) vines were used in basketry and as lashing to build furniture and homes.
- In North America, Indigenous peoples paid attention to how fire inspired growth, and discovered that utilizing controlled burning encouraged certain plants to grow, helped to manage ecosystems, and reduced the risk of large, destructive fires. This is a practice that is being brought back today across many countries, such as Canada, the United States, Australia, Portugal, Spain, France, and South Africa, to prevent out of control fires and to more naturally mimic the ebb and flow of natural ecosystems.

- A more modern invention, the hook-and-loop fastener known as Velcro was inspired by the tenacity and "stickiness" of the hooked, seed-containing burrs of the Burdock (*Arctium lappa*) plant, pictured below, which stick to everything, especially your pet's fur!

As we study plant history, there is no disputing the ability of plants to adapt. Although some plants possess more aggressive natures, the majority of plant species thrive through cooperation. Plants teach us that diversity creates stability. Monocultures—vast plantings of a single species over a large area—are weak and susceptible to disease and extinction. Many famine events throughout history have taught us that relying solely on one type of food crop is dangerous because a single insect swarm can wipe out an entire plant species in one season. Likewise, when forests are replanted with a single type of tree, they fail to thrive and are often seriously damaged by storms and insect invasions.

Because plants can teach us how to live and thrive in a dramatically changing material world, they can teach us on other levels as well. Plants have wisdom to share about the issues that challenge us, whether those be on a personal or global level and whether they relate to our physical, emotional, mental, or spiritual lives. Humans have been relying on plants for this type of wisdom for countless generations.

Plant–Human Relationships

Ethnobotany is the study of how humans across varying geographical locations utilize plants for food, ceremony, healing, artistic expression, and communing with the divine, and the cultural significance of this.

The history of human and plant relationships is a long and diverse one, estimated to be as old as humanity itself. Throughout the distant and recent past, humanity has relied immensely on plants to bring about physical, emotional, and spiritual healing. Recently discovered archeological evidence dating back 60,000 years illustrates the enduring relationship between humans and medicinal plants. In 2012, evidence was unearthed at El Sidrón Cave in northern Spain to suggest that early Neanderthals used herbs such as Yarrow (*Achillea millefolium*), pictured right, and Chamomile (*Matricaria chamomilla*), as well as a fungal pathogen, *Penicillium rubens*, to treat infection.

Through a variety of written historical documents, it is evident that the practice of herbalism has spanned nearly every continent (save Antarctica), every country, every dialect—literally the entire globe.

- The ancient Egyptians used herbs in everything from embalming fluids to complex medicinal formulas, many of which are still in use today.
- The knowledge and energetic practices used by the ancient Greeks remain at the core of many herbal traditions.
- The ancient Romans called upon their herbal knowledge to prepare for battle and utilized it to treat the wounded on the battlefield.
- In Africa, herbal priestesses and traditional medicine women have long held sacred knowledge of plants, blending healing with spiritual and ancestral practices.
- Among Indigenous peoples of North America, medicine women, medicine men, and healers cultivated deep, reciprocal relationships with Plant Allies, guided by ceremony, dreams, and the teachings of the land itself. Their practices were (and remain) holistic, integrating physical, emotional, and spiritual dimensions of healing.

This archetype of the plant healer is global. Together, these healers form an unbroken lineage of relationship with the green world, one that is not confined by borders or written language, but carried in the heart, the hands, and the breath of the Earth herself. The specific remedies, treatments, ceremonies, and rituals in which people heal with plants can vary tremendously from country to country, tradition to tradition, and from individual to individual, but the one main consistency is the sustained engagement of plants in healing traditions.

The Consciousness of Plants

Plants are sentient beings with a demonstrated level of consciousness, yet for many decades, science has largely ignored this possibility. Early visionaries like Charles Darwin recognized the intelligence of plant life, conducting experiments to demonstrate it. In *The Power of Movement in Plants*, Darwin compares the intelligence of plants to that of animal species. He observed that the tip of the main root, or radicle, has the ability to sense its environment, make decisions, and take action based on promoting its survival and desire to flourish. He even went so far as to consider the radicle a type of "brain."

Darwin noted that the radicle is aware of light, moisture, gravity, obstacles, and chemicals, and will alter its behavior accordingly. For instance, experiments showed that the radicle moves toward water sources and away from hard surfaces that impede growth or cause injury; it bends away from light but grows toward gravity. These observations illustrate that plants are aware of their environments; they feel, and they continuously respond to stimuli in much the same way humans and animals do.

More recent scientific discoveries have expanded our understanding of this awareness, highlighting the sophisticated means through which plants communicate with one another and with other species.

- Via mycorrhizal networks—the vast underground fungal webs that connect plant roots—plants report on their environments, sharing water and nutrients, and even exchange chemical warnings.

- Plants release volatile organic compounds (VOCs)—small, lightweight, airborne particles—to convey messages. For example, when under attack by insects, a plant can signal nearby neighbors, prompting them to alter their chemistry to resist the invasion.
- While many flowering plants, such as Lavender (*Lavandula* species), pictured right, emit sweet, alluring scents to attract bees, butterflies, and other pollinators, others such as the Corpse Flower (*Titan arum*) release sulfuric odors that mimic rotting meat to draw in flies and beetles. This dance of communication reveals a world where plants are not passive, but dynamically engaged in relationships of mutualism, attraction, and defense.

- Recent studies indicate that plants emit sounds, not metaphorically, but biologically. Certain species produce ultrasonic clicks or pops when under stress, such as when experiencing drought or damage. Tomato (*Solanum lycopersicum*) and Tobacco (*Nicotiana* species) plants have been observed releasing these vibrations, which other nearby plants may perceive and react to, altering their behavior as if in response to a cry. Roots may even follow the faint sound of flowing water, growing in its direction. This acoustic sensitivity suggests that plants communicate not only through chemicals and light, but also through vibrational resonance, a kind of *rooted listening*.

If we listen closely, we may discover that the world is far more alive than we were taught to believe. In every leaf that turns toward the Sun, in every root that seeks the song of water beneath the soil, there is awareness. Not human awareness but something older, slower, and deeply attuned to the rhythms of Earth. Plants do not speak our language, but they whisper in color, scent, vibration, movement, and growth. They teach not through domination, but through relationship, through mutual thriving. And when we open ourselves to their presence, they do more than grow around us; they grow with us, and within us, inviting us into a profound, more reciprocal way of being.

The consciousness of plants may not be easily measured, but it can be deeply felt. It lives in the way the perfumed bouquet of a Wild Rose (*Rosa* species) travels on the breeze, the way a Sunflower (*Helianthus annuus*) turns its head to face the Sun as it moves across the sky, the way a Dandelion (*Taraxacum officinale*), pictured right, releases her seeds to the wind, the way Mugwort (*Artemisia vulgaris*) guides the dreamer across the veil. To honor this consciousness is to remember that we are not separate from nature; we are part of this thinking, feeling, evolving being.

How Plants Speak to Us

Stepping into the world of plant communication requires a shift in consciousness; an openness to learning and experiencing how plants share their wisdom. If we expect communication with plants to mirror a human conversation, we may miss the message entirely, feel disappointment, or unknowingly project our own desires onto them.

The first step in cultivating an authentic exchange is learning a different kind of language, one that exists beyond the verbal forms we've been conditioned to rely on. To communicate with plants, we must approach them with reverence, humility, and respect for their life force and autonomy.

Plants communicate in ways and across ranges far broader than what our typical senses perceive. To attune to this, we must quiet our often-busy minds and gently expand our field of awareness. As we do so, we transcend the boundaries of ordinary perception, engaging with worlds previously unknown to us. In this illumined state, we awaken to subtler frequencies, stretching the edges of the known world and of our own capacities to listen, feel, and connect.

Plants speak in a language older than words, through light, sound, felt sensation, and what we might call an inner knowing or sixth sense, the quiet stirrings of the soul. Plants reach across spectrums of light and vibration we barely perceive, dancing with frequencies of color and tone that lie just beyond our sight and hearing. To meet them in this sacred space, we must stretch our awareness beyond the edges of the known.

This is the work of becoming porous, of letting the veil thin between our senses and the familiar world. It is an attunement, a remembering. The more we sit with the plants, not to harvest or name them, but to simply *be*, the more our intuition begins to bloom like a wildflower in spring. Transmissions from plants can sometimes feel subtle and dreamlike. Other times, they can be directed toward us with surprising speed and clarity, like a lightning bolt.

In stillness, a subtle exchange begins to unfold.
And in that silence, the plants begin to speak.

Light and Symbols

When plants communicate via light frequency, it is most often in the form of images, pictures, or symbols received telepathically. These appear in our mind's eye or inner vision. Symbolism is multilayered and communicates with more depth and meaning than words can possibly convey. Symbols are timeless and even those messages we received some time ago take on new depth and bring additional insights with the passage of time. These types of communications are remarkable and continue to ripple throughout our consciousness long after they arrive.

The idea of plants communicating via symbol is not a new one. Historically, ancient people around the world believed that plants did, in fact, communicate via symbol. They felt that we could learn the medicinal and other healing properties of local flora by paying attention to specific and notable characteristics they displayed. The Doctrine of Signatures is a concept that holds that the features or "signatures" of plants—their shape, color, texture, growth pattern, the climate and habitat in which they grow, and their proximity to humans—are symbolic in that they resemble, in some way, the condition or body part that the plant can treat. This doctrine is generally attributed to Paracelsus (born Philippus Aureolus Theophrastus Bombastus von Hohenheim), a Swiss physician and alchemist in the sixteenth century, but the concept goes back much earlier to ancient times.

Other cultures have similar beliefs but view these characteristics through different lenses, such as comparing plant attributes to specific animals and their personalities. Some Indigenous peoples in North America speak of certain herbs and healing plants as having a unique "animal medicine," such as Bear or Deer medicine. Bear medicine plants tend to have furry, oily roots and will often strengthen the adrenals and improve overall bodily health. Conversely, Deer medicine plants are often those that are gentle, cooling, and astringent (causing a tightening of certain body tissues, where needed); plants such as Yarrow (*Achillea millefolium*) tend to the heart and are medicines often grazed on by Deer.

Appearance and Location

In our interactions with the green beings, we attune to how they appear and where they choose to grow, each detail part of their ongoing communication with us. Plants that grow abundantly, especially near human dwellings, are often those most eager to work with us and perhaps those we most need. It is an old herbalist's saying that "the plants we need the most are growing right outside our door."

Think of the humble Dandelion (*Taraxacum officinale*), ever-present in lawns, gardens, and the cracks of city sidewalks. She offers herself freely as food, medicine, and as a gentle teacher. In contrast, the plants we must journey to find, those hidden in wild places or blooming only in certain seasons, often carry a different kind of medicine. These are the ones we may work with less frequently, yet their gifts can be profound. Some possess almost mystical qualities, capable of transporting our consciousness to other realms and revealing the unseen. One such being is the Ghost Plant (*Monotropa uniflora*)—my first encounter with this plant is described on page 26.

THE WISDOM OF GHOST PLANT

Unlike most plants, the Ghost Plant, also known as Ghost Pipe, does not draw life from the Sun. Instead, she emerges pale and luminescent from the shaded forest floor, nourished by mycorrhizal networks hidden beneath the soil. Her appearance is rare and quiet, offering herself only to those who approach with stillness and heart.

Ghost Plant is a threshold guide, a spirit ally for the in-between places. Her medicine opens the doors to peace, not just within ourselves, but for those who have passed beyond the veil and have not yet found their way. She offers a deep calm within the soul, assisting in the release of what no longer belongs, helping both the living and the departed find rest and reunion. With her, communication is not loud; it is reverent, luminous, and unmistakably sacred. She reminds us that some messages are meant to be whispered, and some healing happens in the silence between worlds.

The first time Ghost Plant appeared to me was not in a dream, but in the hush of the early morning woods. The light hadn't yet pierced the canopy, and the air carried the weight of mist and memory. Rising ghost-white from the forest floor, she stood in quiet radiance, like a breath made visible. I knelt beside her, unsure whether I had found her, or she had found me.

That day, I wasn't alone in the woods, though no other human walked with me. I had sensed a presence for days, a spirit clinging softly to the edges of this world. As I sat with Ghost Plant, heart open and unguarded, a wave of peace moved through me. It was as though the plant became a lantern, illuminating a path unseen. I offered my prayers and breath, and in the space between moments, I felt the spirit lift, gracefully, gently crossing into the place beyond. Ghost Plant did not speak in words. She did not need to. Her presence was the message, and her medicine was release.

Sound

Many times, when we sit with a plant or walk along a peaceful woodland or garden path, we hear the plants' whispers as sounds like tinkling bells, singing, laughter, or occasionally even a voice. Plants emit vibrations in ranges that can be detected by other plants, insects, and animals but are normally outside of the range of human hearing. As we continue to spend regular time in deep meditation and reflection with the Green Ones, without an agenda or specific goal in mind, we stretch into our own ranges of perception, hearing things we would normally miss in our busy day-to-day lives. These sounds may be perceived in our inner world, or we may even hear them auditorily.

Prior to crafting herbal remedies (see pages 88–91 and 94–97), I will often sit with a plant in meditation, offering up feelings of gratitude for their gentle healing ways and conversation on how I would like to offer their healing magic. When I am crafting herbal remedies, I find myself wandering into a dreamlike state. In this frequency, I often hear tones of the plants that I sing back to them. In these moments, I am acting as a conduit to bring their love into the world in the form of healing herbal teas and remedies. Other times, their healing comes through as energetic frequencies sent to others or to our world as a whole.

Scent

Another way the green world reaches out to us is through scent. Have you ever found yourself walking through a field, a verdant forest, your garden or conservatory, and felt a scent reach out to you seemingly from nowhere? As if the scent itself were an invisible hand from the green world, beckoning you out of your daydream, inviting you into deeper communion? I've had this experience many times, but one of the most notable was when I met Sweetfern (*Comptonia peregrina*).

THE FRAGRANCE OF SWEETFERN

I was hiking one lovely late spring day with a group of friends. Our hike took us through an open forested area with trees of Red Maple (*Acer rubrum*), Sweet Birch (*Betula lenta*), White Birch (*Betula papyrifera*), and Mountain Laurel (*Kalmia latifolia*). As we traveled through an area of meadow, I was overcome by the most hypnotic scent, a stunning combination of herbaceous and spicy vanilla. Unsure which plant was emitting the smell, I was the only person in the group who noticed the fragrance.

With a repeated trip to the area, I found out this lovely plant was Sweetfern; not a fern at all but a deciduous shrub with a musky vanilla scent that was clearly reaching out to me! Sweetfern has since become a beloved Plant Ally of mine whose scent certainly factors into our communications and interactions together.

Wordlessness

Wordless communication is a language beneath language. It is something you may not consciously practice every day, yet have undoubtedly experienced. Think back to a significant relationship in your life, someone with whom a single glance carried volumes. No words were needed and yet understanding traveled between you. The exchange was subtle, but unmistakable. It moved like wind between trees: quiet, alive, and deeply real.

Wordlessness is felt in the heart. It's the way you understand a beloved child's emotions before they've learned to speak, or the way your animal companion looks into your eyes, and you just know—a flick of an ear, a tilt of the head, a leaning closer. All speak without speaking. You know their moods, their longings, their joy. And you respond, instinctively. This is communication that bypasses the tongue and travels through presence.

This is not unlike communicating with plants. The cues may be different, arriving not as expressions, but as impressions—a sudden warmth in your chest, a breeze that rises just as you ask a question, movement in response to a prayer or blessing, or a scent, a memory, or an image that unfurls in your mind's eye when you sit beside Mugwort (*Artemisia vulgaris*) or lean your hand against a Birch (*Betula* species). These are not accidents, they are responses.

PRACTICE

Listening with the Whole Body

Plants speak in vibration, in energy, in subtle resonance. They don't "talk," but they transmit. And to receive these transmissions, we must remember a way of listening that is not with the ears, but with the whole body.

This practice can be done indoors or outdoors, just make sure it is somewhere comfortable and quiet. All you will need is a plant—this can be any type of plant, such as a houseplant, a plant in your yard, or one in a park or other place of nature.

1 Sit with the plant—not to study it, but to *be with it.* Soften. Breathe. Listen with your whole being.

2 Notice the sensations in your body, the way your breath moves, relaxes, and expands. Be aware of any changes in your hands, feet, or other area of your body. Perhaps you feel a tingling sensation or a subtle change of temperature.

3 Notice any shifts in light or color and become aware of any smells around you.

4 Allow any thoughts or feelings to arise or stir within you.

Don't force connection. Let the plant lead. Often, the first language a plant offers is silence. And in that silence, something ancient stirs, an invitation to return to a way of knowing we carried before language, before separation.
A way of belonging.

Awareness and Deep Listening

Learning to still ourselves enhances our ability to receive the subtle messages plants offer. Though their communication may not arrive in words or outward signs, a profound exchange is taking place, one that moves beneath thought, into the quiet soil of conscious awareness.

By cultivating deep listening, we begin to perceive these messages more clearly and with greater accuracy. The field of our awareness opens like a blossom to the Sun and we feel this connection down to our bones. Deep listening requires us to quiet the noise of distraction and become more attuned to the present moment. Stillness can be cultivated through extended meditation, time in nature, or brief moments of conscious breathing throughout the day. The key is consistency, not necessarily duration.

Deep listening begins by listening within. And in that quiet, we discover that the line between ourselves and the green world is not a boundary, but a bridge. There is no single path to awareness. Each person must find the doorway that opens for them, but the practice on pages 32–33 is a good place to start.

PRACTICE

Going Within

This practice is simple but powerful, like the whisper of a leaf before the wind stirs it. It can be done anywhere—in the garden, on a forest trail, or even inside your home—in just five minutes, to help deepen your capacity to listen.

1 Find a quiet place or simply become quiet where you are. Sit or stand comfortably, with your feet touching the Earth or floor.

2 Close your eyes if you feel safe to do so and begin by noticing your breath. Let it deepen naturally, there's no need to force it.

3 As thoughts arise, imagine them as leaves floating down a stream. Let them pass. Don't hold or chase them.

4 Bring your attention to your heart space. Breathe *into* it, as though your heart itself is breathing.

5 Feel deep within your own being, which connects with your inner spirit. Feel into the steady and silent presence within—this presence that is the core of your soul, the truth of who you are.

6 Remain in this state of open attention for as long as you like—just five minutes is enough to shift your state and invite deeper connection.

The more we return to this still point within, the more we remember who we are beneath the noise—a being capable of sensing, receiving, and communing beyond words. From this place of inner clarity, connection with the plant world and all beings becomes natural. It is no longer something we reach for, but something we *remember*.

Plant Allies

If you've ever studied or practiced herbalism or shamanism, you may have heard the term "Plant Ally." Most often the phrase is used in a generic way to refer to all plants one might work with for healing. In truth, the meaning of this term is significantly more specific and moving in its definition and scope.

Although the origin of the term itself is rooted in more recent spiritual traditions, combining the modern shamanistic movement and wise woman traditions, the concept is quite ancient. Elders from ancestral traditions around the world have long understood that plants possess a spirit and a consciousness and have the ability to communicate with humans and other beings. These elders related to and practiced with plants as allies, teachers, and guides, bestowing upon them deep honor and respect—approaching them was done with reverence and ceremony, with songs and gifts of love and affection, illustrating the commitment they had to these sacred bonds.

What is a Plant Ally?

A Plant Ally is a special plant that is specifically attuned to you, and you to them. It may be a plant that:

- Has played an important role in your life, such as a medicinal herb that had a profound impact on your physical health, maybe even providing a key piece in resolving a serious illness or chronic condition.
- Has soothed your emotions or calmed your stress.
- You have a great love for, filling you with an almost unearthly joy.
- You are inexorably drawn to.
- Has inspired your creativity and blessed you with ideas for artistic creations or healing herbal remedies.

A Plant Ally may first reveal itself in the dreamtime, offering otherworldly experiences, messages, or sensations that linger upon waking. Or it may appear again and again in the waking world, following us in subtle ways, showing up near where we live, work, or often travel. Sometimes it's a plant we've always felt a quiet fascination for, without knowing why. Other times, it's one we feel consistently drawn to through gardening, art, or repeated encounters in the natural world. It may call to us with a strong desire to learn its name, its medicine, its spirit. These are the plants that reach toward us as much as we reach toward them.

Our Relationships with Plant Allies

The Plant Ally relationship is based on a sacred trust, one of mutual respect and reciprocity. It is a relationship like any other in that it requires attention and consistency. Taken seriously and treated with love and care, these relationships can change throughout our lives and even grow richer and deeper with the passage of time. In Chapter 3, I will introduce you to some of my many Plant Allies and the wisdom they have shared with me.

Like power animals (spirit guides in animal form), Plant Allies accompany us throughout our lives, guiding us through challenging times, offering a loving hand, a grounding and calming presence. They provide insight into the trials we face along our soul's path and even protection through more precarious adversities. Plant Allies accompany us on our shamanic journeys (see pages 62–71), whispering ancient wisdom as they lead us through the unseen realms. Unlike power animals, Plant Allies are more accessible to us in the physical realm, and through their wisdom, powers for healing, and life cycles, they become a remarkable force for transformative renewal, reconnecting us with ourselves, the Earth, and the sacred rhythms of life.

Discovering a Plant Ally

What a joy it is to discover a Plant Ally, a sacred companion unlike any other. This is not just a friendship, but a soul-knowing, a bond rooted in the unseen. Plants see us clearly. They know us to the depth of our being, our beauty, our wounds, our contradictions. And still, they stand beside us. They do not judge or turn away. They offer their presence, their medicine, their love … just as we are. To be known like this is rare. To be loved like this, rarer still.

There is often a sense of recognition when a Plant Ally comes into our lives, a feeling that goes beyond logic and speaks directly to the heart. The connection may be soft and subtle, or bold and insistent, but it is always meaningful.

Here are some gentle questions to help you begin to recognize your own Plant Ally:

- Is there a plant that keeps appearing to you—in dreams, on walks, in unexpected places?
- Have you always felt drawn to a particular herb, tree, or flower without quite knowing why?
- Is there a plant that seems to "follow" you, showing up where you live, work, or travel?
- Which plant brings you a sense of calm, curiosity, or deep remembrance?
- When you're in nature, which plant do you feel most at home beside?

Take a moment to sit with these questions. Write down any impressions, memories, or feelings that arise. There are no wrong answers, only the slow unfolding of a relationship already in bloom.

In Chapter 2, we will explore a variety of practices for communicating with plants and our Plant Allies. Many of these exercises are not just about communication; they will be leading us into luminous spirit-to-spirit connections and through these experiences, we delightfully discover our plant kin.

While I may refer to the plants we work with as Plant Allies, it is not at all necessary to have identified a Plant Ally before practicing plant communication. In fact, it is through practicing many of the exercises in this book that you will discover who your Plant Ally or Allies are. Often, these special bonds develop over time like many of our human relationships do. Other times, the knowing is unmistakable; a cosmic magnetism that can't be denied. However they weave their way into your consciousness, these are precious and beloved connections to be loved and treasured.

MY SUGAR MAPLE TREE ALLY

One of my earliest memories of my kinship with my green friends came when I was young, perhaps eight years old or even younger. I was very fond of climbing trees. I climbed all the trees in our yard whose branches I could reach. For some, I had to devise plans on how to get to those first branches. Naturally, I had my favorites; my friends that I returned to over and over. One of those, a best friend if you will, was a beloved Sugar Maple tree (*Acer saccharum*) that I spent hours sitting in, hoisting up books that I would read among the branches. I would literally spend hours there.

I could feel those branches holding me and I knew that in that tree I was safe. As it was, I fell out of the tree a couple of times and yet, despite its considerable height, I always seemed to land safely, a branch appearing out of nowhere to block my fall. My earliest recollections of communications with this tree were of the tree "telling" me that when a tree of a particular species knew you and was your friend, then all the trees of that species would recognize you as a friend. This is as true for me today as it was then—I always feel an energy of recognition and fondness with this tree species.

Honoring the Plant Spirits

The bond we share with our Plant Allies is built on a timeless trust—a sacred, evolving partnership that has the power to transform our lives in profound ways. These green beings are more than medicines; they are spiritual mentors, teachers, and dear friends. How we treat them directly affects the quality of our communications with them.

Just as we respond to love and care, so too do the plants. The more consistently and heartfully we honor them, the deeper our connection becomes. Gratitude opens pathways. The more we recognize their presence and gifts, the more synchronicities arise. These encounters are not coincidences; they are reminders that something ancient is being remembered.

When we bring our own offerings to the plants—not just in ritual, but in the way we walk the Earth—we shift the dynamic from one of consumption to one of reciprocity. It is no longer a one-way path of taking but a shared journey of giving and receiving. So how do we honor and give back to the plants? What touches their spirits? What makes them smile through their leaves?

When we think of what might be important to the Plant Spirits, the first thing that should come to mind is autonomy and respect. In a world that views plants as non-verbal and therefore without presence or intelligence, humans have a tendency to do with plants what they will. Our first task in learning to honor the Green Ones is to shift our perception of them and respect their autonomy as unique individuals. We need to learn to ask their permission for actions that will affect them and not take their participation as a given.

PRACTICE

Restore Your Connection with the Plant Spirits

In this exercise, you will learn to reach out with love and intention to create a new and renewed bond with the Plant Spirits, one based on mutual esteem and trust. It will take 5–10 minutes and can be performed indoors or outdoors, in a quiet, private area where you will not be disturbed. It will be helpful to have a notebook with you.

1 If you are indoors, you may want to light a candle and burn incense.

2 Take a few deep and cleansing breaths, clearing your mind and centering yourself in the moment.

3. Place your focus on your heart, feeling into your energetic and emotional heart space. Explore what it means to you to restore this sacred connection with the Green Ones. Really feel into this space, acknowledging how much you want to reignite this sacred covenant.

4. When you feel clear on your intention, send this feeling from your heart space out to all the Plant Spirits. You may see it going out as a white light or energy, or your perception may be more of a feeling. See your message and soulful intention being received.
5. Spend a few moments in silence and reverence. Notice any stirrings or feelings that arise.
6. Jot down any insights or messages you may have received.

As you go about your day after this exercise, pay attention to any synchronicities, thoughts, or feelings that come back to you.

Know that the Plant Spirits have heard your call and will respond accordingly.

Create a Plant Altar

As your relationship with the Plant Spirits develops, you may feel called to create a space in your home to honor them—a small altar or sacred corner where your connection can take root and grow. A plant altar is not about decoration; it is about devotion. It's a place to offer gratitude, to listen, to connect. Let it be a reflection of your connection, one that shifts and blooms with the seasons of your spirit.

You might place on it a photo or drawing of a Plant Ally, a small bundle of dried leaves, a flower essence, or a piece of bark gifted from the forest. Stones, crystals, candles, feathers, and bowls of water may also find their way there, each one an offering and a reminder of the sacredness woven through your everyday life. Tending this space can be part of your Plant Spirit practice.

Once you have created your special place, you may want to use the Altar Dedication Blessing on the next page to mark the occasion. Speak this blessing aloud or silently to yourself to set your intention for this space.

Altar Dedication Blessing

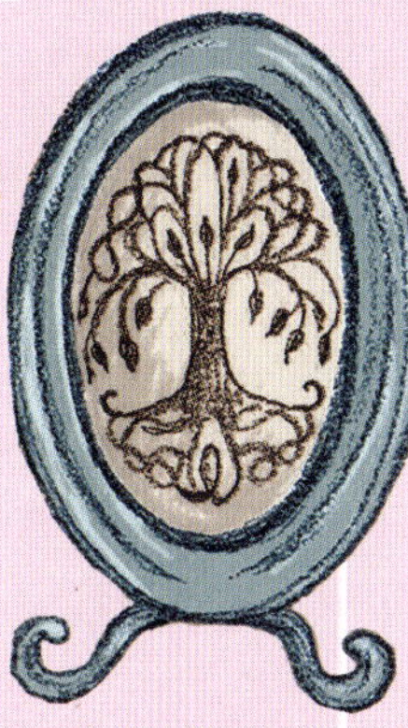

I dedicate this space to the Green Ones.
To the whisper of leaves,
The breath of roots,
The songs of unseen spirits.

May this altar be a place of peace,
A place of presence,
A place of deep listening.

I welcome the Plant Spirits here,
As teachers, as allies, as beloved kin.
May this space honor our connection.
May my heart remain open to your guidance.

With gratitude, with humility, with love …
I offer this space back to the Earth,
In beauty, in balance, in grace.

Protect Their Homes

Creating space for the plants to thrive and protecting their homes are other critical ways to bless the Spirits of the Plants. As a shamanic plant practitioner and herbalist, I have forever been instructing students to leave at least a portion of the areas where they live "wild." I recognize that this can be difficult to do in some locations because townships often have rules about lawn heights and specific standards regarding the maintenance of yards. But if we make the effort, we often find ways to accomplish this manifest, even if in some small way. The plants appreciate our sincere efforts, and amazing things happen when we take action or, at other times, take no action.

Movements like "No Mow May"—in which mowing is postponed throughout the month of May to let pollinators "wake up"—allow for change in how we view the Earth under our care. As we participate in these new ways of thinking and behaving, the plants respond in kind. One of the first things we notice is that the plants begin to show up! Some of them we may have never seen before, while others have been a part of the land for eons, waiting for the opportunity to make their presence known again. Beautiful meadows and forested areas rich with biodiversity are waiting to return and take their place once again in the world of form.

If we cannot leave all the land under our care to its own devices, we can consider leaving a section untampered with, perhaps a small place in our backyard or an area between neighboring landscapes. Even a pot on a deck or balcony will often sprout unknown plants, bursting forth from a seed dropped by a passing bird or other animal.

Get to Know Them

Learning the plants' names and discovering everything about them is another way to show gratitude for their life force. Similarly, when we are interested in getting to know another human, we make the effort to learn about them, to learn their name, their likes and dislikes. We want to know their story. Plants all have stories, too. Stories of where in the world they originated, how they came to be where you have met them, what type of habitat they prefer, and who their friends are. As we learn to sit and listen to the plants with an open and sincere heart, they will share their stories with us.

Attend to Their Needs

Taking care of a plant's needs is a beautiful and loving way to honor their being. I have a deep and personal relationship with a local native plant that lives in a park near me. One very hot summer, we went through several weeks with no rain whatsoever. This plant is native to moist, woodland environments and was beginning to dry out and wither in the sustained heat. I began to arrive daily with water and prayers for her survival. Sure enough, she did wither a bit, but her overall being survived and thrived on into the next seasons and is continuing to thrive today.

Sing or Play Music to Them

Another way we can honor the Plant Spirits is through music and song. Plants love to be sung to! Students often worry about the quality of their singing voices, but the plants only care about your intention. They know your heart so when you approach them in a heartfelt way, they recognize it immediately. You can craft a simple song of your love and appreciation for the plants or simply intone to them from your heart center (see pages 78–79).

If you are musically inclined, you can play your music for them. Plants appreciate live music of flutes, rattles, drums, and any other instrument you can think of. As you play for them, pay attention to any movement or swaying the plant may exhibit. This is a sign that they are acknowledging and appreciate your love in this form.

Send Healing Frequencies to Them

If you are an energy healer or reiki practitioner, you can send healing frequencies to the entire plant kingdom, to the plants in your yard or neighborhood, or to a specific Plant Ally. These energetic gifts help the plants grow and thrive and are highly appreciated.

Reiki or other healing modalities, such as Integrated Energy Therapy, can be performed at any time. Prepare yourself as you normally would for giving an energy healing session—this should include grounding and centering yourself, clearing your mind, and setting up sacred space. If the plant you are sending healing frequencies to is local, you can visit the plant in person. If the plant is not within physical reach, the healing modality can be sent over a distance, either by having a vision in your mind or a photograph or other representation (see pages 98–99) for this purpose.

As we would customarily do as healing practitioners, always ask the plants' permission before doing any energy healing. To do this, become quiet, going within to center yourself. First, send out your intention to do energy healing for this particular plant or plant species, asking if this is appropriate to do so at this time. Direct your intention and question to the Plant Spirit directly, or to the universe, if that feels right. Become still and listen with your whole being to feel what comes back to you in the way of an answer. No matter what it is, honor that as you would when asking permission to work with a human.

If the answer is "no," remember there can be many reasons for this response that have nothing to do with you. Sometimes, the "no" really means "not right now." You can resend the request at a later time and see if the response changes. At times in my life, I have sat with plants that I wanted to engage with but it didn't feel like the right time, or I reached out and felt like the response was unclear. In these cases, I would always wait. In most instances, the moment came when it *was* time to embrace a meaningful connection, but in some instances, the time didn't arrive (at least not yet anyway). These were plants that I have not developed deeper relationships with, and I accept that. Just like we're not meant to be "friends" with everyone, not every Plant Spirit will be one that we will dance with.

When you receive a "yes" or affirmative response, conduct the healing session as you normally would, making sure to close the energetic connection when you have completed your session. Jot down in your notebook any insights or revelations.

Make Offerings to Them

Like most people, plants love gifts. Although we may refer to them as offerings, they are presents of love and affection, an acknowledgment of all that the plants give to us so generously and the many ways they enrich our lives. Offerings can take many forms. In some cultures, it is traditional to give small amounts of Tobacco (*Nicotiana* species) or Cornmeal (*Zea mays*), or we can offer small crystals. Even water, which is precious to plants' survival, can be an appreciated offering. Physical offerings should be given with care and reverence and gently left just below or near the plant.

Gifts that you have crafted yourself will always be gratefully received by the plants. Conjuring poetry, songs, works of art, and drawings in their likeness are beautiful ways to hold their presence sacred. Crafting these gifts from the heart will open the pathways of communion like no other, and setting aside time to bring forth these precious treasures creates energetic pathways that will connect you with your plant friend. Share your works of art with others to inspire them to develop their own appreciation and relationship with these special beings.

Pray with Them

Prayer can be a beautifully simple and poignant offering of our love and awe. Prayer, in this context, is not something directed *to* the plants, but rather offered *in their presence*. It is a gesture of reverence, a way of expressing gratitude, humility, and love for the beings who live beside us in green silence. When we include plants in our prayers, we are not worshipping them, but honoring their wisdom, their generosity, and their role in our shared path.

Prayer becomes a bridge, an offering from the heart that acknowledges the unseen threads between us. It can be as simple as a whispered thank you, a song sung softly to the soil, or a breath of presence shared before harvest. In this way, prayer becomes an act of listening, not asking; a reciprocal moment of connection that deepens the relationship between plant and person.

Through these prayerful exchanges, we align our spirit with theirs, remembering that we are not separate from the Earth but part of a vast and living web, where every being has a voice, and every voice is worthy of being heard. These are all the foundations and beginning chords of hearing the plants' songs.

A Prayer of Offering to the Plant Spirits

I come to you with an open heart filled with gratitude,
And a spirit willing to listen.

Thank you for your presence,
For your teachings,
And for the life you share so generously.

May I walk gently beside you,
In respect, in care, in kinship.

I offer this moment, this breath, this gratitude,
Not as a request,
But as a remembrance.

We are part of each other.
I see you.
And I thank you.

CHAPTER 2

PRACTICES FOR COMMUNICATING WITH PLANTS

There are many ways to communicate with plants. In this chapter, I share a variety of practices that I, and others, have found to carry deep resonance with the Divine Spirits of the Plants. Some of these techniques may feel natural and familiar to you, while others may feel new or unfamiliar, and that's perfectly okay.

Preparing to Communicate with Plants

Plant communication is most effective when we come to it with presence and clarity. If you're feeling scattered, distracted, or emotionally unsettled, the messages may feel distant or unclear. Some of the communication techniques in this chapter, such as shamanic journeying (pages 62–71) and various meditations (pages 54–61), are multilayered practices with many meanings. Preparing ourselves for successful communication is therefore of the utmost importance. The following tips will help you to prepare and get the most out of the practices in this chapter.

- **Rather than pushing through, pause:** We want to clear our minds and be in the proper state for communication, allowing enough time to fully embrace the experience. Take some deep breaths or spend a few quiet moments journaling to release what may be clouding your mind. You could go for a gentle walk in nature or sit in silence with a favorite tree or plant to help you reset. These small acts of preparation open the heart and quiet the mind, allowing for a more reverent exchange. This is not about perfection, it's about presence. The plants are patient. They will meet you where you are, as long as you come with sincerity and care.

- **Keep a notebook:** As you engage with the exercises and your interactions with the plants flourish, it's wonderful to have a record of your experiences. Some of the techniques you'll be learning and engaging with can have a daydreamlike quality; in the moments that follow, you may remember them with perfect clarity, but the rich details and messages can fade over time. Writing down your unfolding journeys and experiences with the plants is a great way to remember them and have a record of these growing and evolving relationships. The initial learnings from your interactions will no doubt change over time, so going back and reviewing them can illustrate previously unperceived information and symbolism.
- **Don't try everything at once:** Read through this chapter gently and pay attention to the practices that stir your curiosity or speak to your spirit. Begin there. Let these exercises become your doorway into deeper communion. You can always return later to explore other practices as you feel called. What matters most is finding what resonates for *you*. This is your sacred relationship with the Green Ones, a path of discovery that is uniquely your own.

Meditation

Meditation is one method we can use to connect and communicate with plants. It trains us to slow down our thought processes, allowing us to still our minds. This enhances our ability to become more aware of the subtler energetic vibrations emanating from other life-forms and the atmosphere around us. Meditation is a wonderful practice to employ for a change of pace. If you currently have a meditation practice that you enjoy, it is a natural evolution to bring your plant friends and allies into this process.

The practice on pages 55–56 will walk you through a plant meditation in which you will have the opportunity to meet a Plant Ally. This meditation practice involves creative visualization, which is a guided type of meditation whereby you will follow a preset, scripted narrative in which the visual cues are laid out for you. Utilizing the framework of the narrative journey can create a strong foundation for connecting with the Spirits of the Plants and establishing a relationship with a Plant Ally. In this liminal space, you can connect with any type of Plant Spirit, whether it be a tree, a shrub, a herb, or even an ornamental plant.

Any plant can show up in your meditation. The key is to stay open and trust whatever presents itself to you.

PRACTICE

Sacred Garden Meditation

This meditation will take you to your very own sacred garden. It can be performed anytime and anywhere you like, indoors or outdoors—just make sure it is quiet, and you will not be disturbed. Gather your journal and writing instrument to record your experiences and insights afterward. Read the steps a couple of times beforehand to memorize them or record the words to listen to while you meditate.

1 Settle into a comfortable, seated position you can easily maintain, in which your body is fully supported but relaxed. Close your eyes and take a few deep, cleansing breaths. Bring all your attention to this moment and your breath, feeling the air as it slowly enters your nose and gently fills your lungs. Feel yourself becoming more relaxed with each calm, even exhalation.

2 Scan your body for any areas of tension and send your breath to soothe and soften these places. Continue to focus on your inhalations and exhalations, letting go of any thoughts until your mind becomes still.

3 Now imagine a swirl of soft mist surrounding you, transporting you to the liminal space between ordinary and non-ordinary reality. With each breath, the veil between the worlds begins to thin. Allow yourself to drift gently into a place beyond time; a space where Plant Spirits live and dream.

4 You find yourself standing at the threshold of a garden sanctuary shimmering with life. This is no ordinary garden. It is sacred, woven from memory and soul, and tended to by the spirits of the green world. Look at the path beneath your feet—it may be moss, earthen, or smooth stones. How does it feel? Notice the enchanting scents in the air and the vibrant colors of the plants and flowers blooming everywhere, which have a magical quality, an inner glow that enlivens your senses. Listen to the sounds all around you—trickling water, birdsong, the whispers of unseen beings.

Continued over page

Continued from previous page

5 Let yourself wander slowly through this garden that welcomes you. As you explore, you begin to sense a presence nearby, a particular Plant Spirit who is ready to meet you. It may appear as a plant you recognize, or as a glowing presence or guide. Allow it to approach you. Observe. Feel. Listen. What is its essence? What do you sense in its presence?

6 As you become more comfortable with this plant's energy, ask if there is something it would like to share with you—this might be a message, a gift, a gesture, or simply its presence. Receive what is given with an open heart and gratitude. Although you may not understand it all right now, its wisdom will unfold in time. Ask this plant how you may honor it or, if you like, you can leave a blessing, a prayer, or words of love and gratitude.

7 When your meeting feels complete, thank your ally. Let them know you will carry their teachings with you. Slowly begin to make your way back through the garden, taking with you the feeling of connection and the memory of this place, knowing that you can return. The mist begins to reappear, gently wrapping around you, guiding you back to your waking body.

8 As you reconnect with your physical body, deepen your breath and bring small movements into your fingers and toes. When you're ready, gently open your eyes. You may wish to journal about your experience, sketch the plant you met, or simply sit in stillness and gratitude.

9 After your meditation, give yourself sufficient time to come back to ordinary reality. Drinking water or going for a slow walk will help to ground you.

Tea Meditation

A tea meditation is another, visceral way to communicate with the Spirit of a Plant. Long before tea became a café commodity, and tea-drinking a household ritual, it was a sacred act, an offering, a meditation, a doorway into stillness. Across time and tradition, humans have gathered with warm cups in hand, not just to nourish the body, but to quiet the mind, to honor the moment, and to connect with the essence of the plant and the elements. In temple gardens, mountain hermitages, ancestral kitchens, and forest clearings, tea has served as both medicine and mirror, reflecting the soul

"Drink your tea slowly and reverently,
as if it is the axis on which the world turns."

Thich Nhat Hanh, Vietnamese Buddhist monk

back to itself. Whether crafted with traditional *Camellia sinensis* tea leaves or wild Mugwort (*Artemisia vulgaris*), the act of preparing and drinking tea has carried the essence of reverence. Tea ceremonies and meditations have emerged across cultures as a bridge between the seen and unseen, the ordinary and the sacred.

While many tea meditation practices arise from specific cultural lineages, a growing number of herbalists, healers, and Earth-honoring practitioners are returning to the simple yet profound act of drinking tea as a way to connect deeply with plants and with ourselves. This approach draws inspiration from animistic and Indigenous

THE HISTORY OF TEA DRINKING

The discovery of tea is often attributed to the Chinese Emperor Shen Nung (2737 BCE), who would drink hot water beneath a *Camellia sinensis* tree. One breezy day, several leaves fell into his cup. As the leaves steeped in the water, a mysterious new beverage formed. This magical brew created a strange alertness, which encouraged mindfulness and increased energy but also brought about relaxation. Thus, the practice of drinking tea was born.

In ancient China, tea was more than a beverage, it was a path. Rooted in Daoist philosophy and natural cosmology, the Dao of Tea—mindfully brewing and drinking tea—emphasized harmony with nature, simplicity of action, and the cultivation of inner stillness. Drinking tea was a way to align with the subtle flow of life force (known as *Qi*) and to experience the sacred within the everyday. In Japan, this approach deepened into the practice of *Chadō*, "the Way of Tea," which was heavily influenced by Zen Buddhism. Refined over centuries into a formalized meditative art, the Japanese tea ceremony embraced silence, intention, and grace. Every gesture, every tool, and every breath was a chance to embody presence.

worldviews—traditions that have long recognized plants as sentient beings, healers, and spiritual allies. With deep respect for these lineages and without claiming them, modern practitioners are listening anew, preparing herbal infusions slowly, offering breath and prayer, and receiving the Spirit of the Plant through the body and the heart. In this way, a warm cup becomes a vessel for presence, relationship, and remembrance—a quiet act of devotion that reconnects us with the living world.

Traditionally, the leaves of *Camellia sinensis* have been used for tea ceremonies. This is the tea we've come to know as black tea, green tea, oolong, or white tea—all traditional "tea" comes from this same plant. The differences between these types relate mainly to processing times and methods. Any ingestible herb, such as Chamomile (*Matricaria chamomilla*), Rose (*Rosa* species), Spearmint (*Mentha spicata*), Lemon Balm (*Melissa officinalis*), Dandelion (*Taraxacum officinale*), pictured above, or Mugwort (*Artemisia vulgaris*), pictured below, is appropriate for a tea meditation. (**Safety note:** It is your responsibility to ensure the tea is safe to consume. Seek professional advice if needed. Mugwort should not be ingested during pregnancy or lactation.) A single herb is preferable, rather than a complex blend, in order to focus on the relationship with one plant.

These teas are not merely consumed; they are sipped with intention, felt with the soul, and honored as living beings. Each tea meditation becomes a conversation, an offering, and a return to a sacred relationship with the green world. Sitting in silence with a cup of Mugwort tea may open the doors of inner vision, helping one hear the whisper of a Plant Spirit or receive guidance from the unseen realm. Or if it is Rose that steps forward for you, she offers a softening of the heart, gentle healing, and reminds us of beauty as medicine.

On the following pages, I will guide you through a mindful tea meditation.

PRACTICE

A Mindful Meditative Tea Journey

To enjoy a mindful tea meditation, choose a time and location where you will not be disturbed for at least 5–10 minutes. Read through the instructions beforehand so you can be as present as possible. You will need 8–10 fl oz (240–300 ml) of water, 2–3 teaspoons of loose-leaf tea or herbs, a vessel to boil the water in, one to brew the tea in, such as a teapot or coffee press, and a cup.

1 Place the loose-leaf tea or herbs into your teapot then boil the water in a separate vessel, becoming aware of your movements throughout. Make this an intentional process—notice the color of the tea or herbs and the sensations of the tools in your hands.

2 Carefully pour the boiled water into the teapot. Notice the sounds, the steam rising into the air, the aroma that fills your nose, and the way the color of the water changes as the herbs infuse.

3 Let your tea steep. Traditional teas are usually steeped for 2–3 minutes while a herbal tea is steeped for 10–15 minutes. For specific steeping times, refer to the directions on the packaging.

4 Strain off the herbs and pour the tea into the cup, leaving it to cool to a comfortable drinking temperature.

5 Settle into the place you'll sit then bring your attention to your breath. Allow it to slow, soften, and deepen. With each inhale and exhale, feel yourself relaxing, releasing the outside world and turning inward.

6 Bring the cup into your hands. Feel its shape, its weight, the warmth radiating from within. Let this be your anchor to the present moment. Slowly lift the cup and breathe in the aroma of the tea.

7 Watch the steam curl into the air like an offering. Notice the color and tone of the liquid—the light playing through it and the shadows resting in it. Let yourself become fully immersed in this sensory moment.

8 Take another slow breath in and exhale gently, releasing any thoughts. Then, take a small sip of tea, allowing it to linger on your tongue. Notice its flavor, its texture, its temperature. What does it whisper to your senses?

9 Continue to take small, intentional sips. Set the cup down between sips and sit in stillness. You may notice the flavor begins to evolve or deepen. If your mind wanders, return your attention to the warmth in your hands, the breath in your body, and the spirit of the tea. There is no rush, no goal; just presence.

10 As you continue sipping, you may begin to sense the essence of the plant moving through you quietly, gently, with its own wisdom. Allow yourself to receive, noticing any feelings, images, or subtle impressions that arise. There is nothing you need to do; simply be in relationship.

11 When you've taken your final sip, hold the empty cup in your hands with gratitude. You may wish to close your eyes and send a silent thank you to the plant, to the water, and to the Earth that made this moment possible.

12 Sit for a few more breaths in stillness and let the spirit of the tea settle within you. When you're ready, gently return to your day, carrying this calm, this connection, and this quiet knowing with you.

Shamanic Journeying

We can utilize shamanic journeying to communicate with and learn from plants in our environment or plants we would like to connect with, and to discover Plant Allies. Although the word "shaman" comes from the Tungus people of Siberia, shamanism has been practiced by every culture on every continent in one form or another. In this book, I use the terms "shamanism" and "shamanic" not in relation to a specific culture, but to refer to a technique that can be used to discover and access spiritual information in "non-ordinary" reality, or the spirit world. Through this practice, we enter into a state of perception that is outside of our "ordinary" waking reality.

In ancient civilizations, shamanic techniques were performed for every purpose imaginable: to find food, game, and lost objects, to seek answers to important questions, for rite of passage rituals, and for discovering and creating healing ceremonies. Today, we can engage with shamanic techniques to bring about healing and balance in a number of ways, such as to find answers to deep and personal questions, work through current issues within ourselves, work on our relationships with others (living or deceased), and let go of unhelpful habits and/or create new, more helpful ones.

The shamanic journey is just one aspect of shamanism. It does not represent all the practices that exist within shamanism, but it's one of the more accessible techniques. A shamanic journey can be compared to creative visualization (see page 54), with a few key differences:

- A shamanic journey is a ceremony performed in sacred space.
- It utilizes a percussion instrument or recording (see pages 67–68).
- There is no preset narrative beyond the recommended world in which the journey will take place.
- It is more of a spontaneous experience. Beyond the intent or focus of the journey, which will be unique, the journey can be taken "off script" based on how it unfolds.

Over the next few pages, we will explore these different elements that make up a shamanic journey. The practice on pages 70–71 will enable you to put all of this together and experience a shamanic journey to meet a Plant Ally.

Creating Sacred Space

The first step in the practice of journeying is to create sacred space—this is a space that exists outside of ordinary reality, where the veil thins and we can turn inward without distraction or demand. In the physical sense, this should be a place of quiet and comfort. However, sacred space is not simply a physical place, but a *state of being* we enter with intention and care. In this space, we step away from the noise of daily life and make room for Spirit. Through conscious intention and preparation, we create a container in which we can feel safe, supported, and spiritually held.

The act of setting sacred space is not a formality; it is a powerful invocation. It is how we signal to ourselves and the unseen realms that we are ready to enter the mystery. We do this not only for ourselves, but in remembrance, because this is a sacred inheritance. Every one of us comes from ancestors who, in some form, practiced this kind of soul-travel and spirit communion. And when we journey, we connect not only with our guides and allies, but with our Divine Source and through that, with the eternal spark of Spirit that lives within us.

Smudging and Energetic Preparation

Clearing the space of any stagnant energies, emotional residue, or stress that may interfere with our ability to connect will help to create a space, and a state of mind, that is most conducive to a successful journey. There are many ways to energetically cleanse a space, but one of the most widely used methods in shamanic practice is smudging, which involves burning a small amount of dried, aromatic herbs. This can be done in a heat-safe bowl or container, such as a clay smudge pot or shell. The container is then moved gently through the space and the smoke works to shift and lift the energetic field. See page 64 for steps on how to smudge in this way. Alternatively, you could craft your own smudge bundle (see pages 92–93), which will enhance your connection with the plants used in the bundle.

Other methods for clearing space include the use of bells or chimes, crystals such as clear quartz or selenite, or smudge sprays made with essential oils. These tools can be used in much the same way as traditional smudging. The method matters less than the intention. What's most important is that it leaves you feeling cleansed and grounded.

PRACTICE

Smudging to Cleanse Your Space and Yourself

To smudge, you will need a small bundle or pinch of dried, aromatic herbs, a heat-safe container, and a match or lighter. While White Sage (*Salvia apiana*) has traditionally been used for smudging in many Indigenous practices, it is increasingly at risk in the wild. There are many other beautiful allies you can use instead, such as Garden Sage (*Salvia officinalis*), Lavender (*Lavandula* species), pictured below, or Mugwort (*Artemisia vulgaris*).

1 Place your chosen herbs in the heat-safe container and light the herbs.

2 Gently blow out the flame, allowing the smoke to rise.

3 With intention, pass the smoke through the space, inviting it to clear away what is no longer needed. Focus on doorways, corners, and the area where you will be journeying. Always move with respect and mindfulness; the clearing is energetic as much as it is physical.

4 If you wish, say the following blessing as you move through the space:

With this smoke, I cleanse and clear.
All that is heavy, I release.
All that is sacred, I welcome near.
May this space be pure and protected.
May my heart be open and true.
I walk with Spirit.
I walk with peace.

It's also nourishing to smudge yourself before journeying, or as part of a daily ritual. Follow steps 1 and 2 above then use your hand, a feather, or a smudge fan to waft the smoke around your body, beginning at your feet then moving up your legs, torso, and arms, over the heart, and around the crown of the head. As you do so, let your intention be clear. You could say: "I release what I no longer need. I make space for Spirit."

Calling and Honoring the Directions

The act of calling the directions is a way of honoring their place in our sacred space. Some cultures recognize four directions, each representing one of the four elements: the north signifies Earth, the east Air, the south Fire, and the west Water. I recognize and honor seven directions—these four cardinal directions plus above, below, and within. The "above" and "below" honor Father Sky and Mother Earth, respectively; the "within" represents the Sacred Heart within and our internal connection to the Great Spirit. In your practice, you can choose to honor four directions or more as you feel called. Allow your intuition to guide you, knowing that you can't do this wrong.

There are many ways to call in the directions. In some traditions, practitioners whistle through sacred animal bones. Others may sing, drum, rattle, or speak prayers aloud. I've used a variety of methods depending on the purpose of the journey and the energy I'm working with. Most often, I rattle for each direction, calling them in silently or aloud but always with my heart and attention. If possible, try to physically face each of the directions as you call them.

Each direction holds its own unique power, gifts, wisdom, and presence. When we call to a direction, we offer gratitude and honor each one's presence in turn, inviting its power to join us—to witness, to protect, and to guide. As you move through each direction, let your focus rest on its essence and elemental energy. Make your own prayers, set your own intentions, and invite that direction to infuse your space with its wisdom. There is no one right way to do this; intention is everything. The more you walk this path, the more your own way of calling the directions will reveal itself to you. Trust that. The directions are listening.

SIMPLE INVOCATIONS FOR THE DIRECTIONS

Here are some suggested words you can say, aloud or in your head, to call the directions—four or seven, whichever feels right to you.

North—Earth: Spirit of the north, thank you for bringing grounding, strength, and the guidance of the ancestors.

East—Air: Spirit of the east, thank you for bringing clarity, vision, and new beginnings.

South—Fire: Spirit of the south, thank you for bringing courage, transformation, and the spark of life.

West—Water: Spirit of the west, thank you for bringing healing, intuition, and the deep wisdom of emotion.

Above—Father: Sky Spirit above, thank you for guiding me with light, love, and divine wisdom.

Below—Mother: Earth roots below, thank you for holding me in strength, memory, and the wisdom of those who came before.

Within—Heart/Spirit: Spirit within, thank you for helping me listen with truth, walk with integrity, and speak with love.

Percussion in the Journey

Sound is a sacred ally in shamanic journeying. Whether it's the deep, steady beat of a drum or the crisp rhythm of a rattle, percussion acts as a bridge between worlds, helping us step out of ordinary time and into sacred space. The purpose of percussion is to help shift your awareness, to quiet the thinking mind, and open the inner senses. Over time, your body will learn to recognize these rhythms as the signal to soften, to listen, and to move into the journey space.

A frame drum is widely used in shamanic traditions, but it is not the only path. Rattles, flutes, didgeridoos, and clapsticks can all be used, as can a drum or rattle recording. Use whatever sound feels most resonant for you. What matters is not the instrument, but the intention and the sacred space it opens within you. Turn to page 68 for some tips on how to choose and use your sound.

The instruments are not just tools, they are spirit companions, and should be treated with respect. Play them with reverence, keep them covered when not in use, and store them in a way that honors their sacred purpose. Many practitioners use cloths or cases for their instruments, which hold personal or ceremonial significance.

CHOOSING AND USING YOUR SOUND

There is no single "right" instrument for journeying but some suggestions are outlined below. Let your intention guide you; the spirit world responds most to your heart, not your tools.

- **Frame drum:** A popular choice, a frame drum is simple to play and allows you to easily achieve a monotonous beat. The drumhead is usually made of animal hide but synthetic options are also available. Frame drums are typically 14–20 in (35–50 cm) in diameter; smaller drums generally have a higher pitch while larger drums will have a deeper sound.
- **Rattle:** A powerful, portable ally, you can buy a rattle or make your own by placing seeds, stones, crystals, or shells in a gourd.
- **Recording:** If you don't have a physical instrument, a drum or rattle recording works beautifully. Choose a track with a consistent rhythm (ideally 3–4 beats per second). Avoid layered music or singing until you are more experienced.

Play your instrument in a steady, rhythmic pattern (or listen to a recording) for 10–15 minutes while sitting down. Focus inward while the rhythm supports your descent into the journeying state. If you wish, you can continue to play or listen throughout the journey.

The Three Shamanic Worlds

In a shamanic journey, there are three general areas or directions we can journey to: the Upper World, the Middle World, and the Lower World. Within each world, there is an infinite number of levels, which can differ greatly. If you are new to shamanic journeying, you won't necessarily reach these additional levels, but it is important to be aware of their existence. Each of the three worlds has a very different terrain and feel to it, and can be journeyed to for different purposes.

- **The Upper World** is ethereal and is a place where we find ascended masters, teachers, and the angelic realm. Many people journeying to the Upper World travel through cloud cover or fog before arriving there.
- **The Middle World** is the spiritual dimension of our everyday life and where we conduct healing and healing ceremonies, talk to the spirits of the land, find lost objects, and create ceremony.
- **The Lower World** tends to be earthy, with canyons, fields, forests, and valleys, and is a place where we often discover power animals and other Earth-centered guides, as well as the Spirits of the Plants. The Lower World is a beautiful place to begin when seeking to meet a Plant Ally who is ready to work with you.

PRACTICE

Shamanic Journey to Meet a Plant Ally

You are now ready to embark on a journey to the Lower World to connect with a Plant Ally. Utilize your instrument or recording before starting the journey to aid your mind in reaching the journey state. You can continue to use it throughout the journey, too. Read through the below steps a couple of times before you begin.

1. Imagine a place in nature that feels familiar or comforting to you. It could be somewhere you've visited in waking life or which appears in your dreams. Let yourself settle fully into this landscape, breathing into its atmosphere.
2. Look for an opening in the earth, a doorway into the Lower World. This could be a hollow at the base of a tree, a tunnel in the roots, a cave, a hole in the ground, a spring, or a river. Trust what appears. This is your threshold.
3. Enter the opening and follow the path downward, allowing yourself to be guided into a wild, natural setting. Take your time. Feel the texture beneath your feet. Sense the air, the light, and the energy of this sacred place.
4. As you walk, open your senses fully. Notice what plants appear to you. What do you see growing here? Is there a tree that calls to you, a vine that brushes your arm, a flower that glows with color or scent? You may see animals, too, but keep your focus gently attuned to the green world.
5. If a plant draws your attention, approach it with respect. Sit with it. Notice its features, its feeling, its presence. You may hear words, see images, or simply feel something stir in your heart. Ask the plant, "Are you my ally?" You may receive a clear "yes," a gesture, or simply a feeling of warmth or invitation. If not, continue walking until one reveals itself.
6. Once you've found a Plant Spirit that wishes to work with you, spend time together. Ask how you are meant to work with them, and what they wish to teach you. Listen deeply. There may be medicine, song, insight, or even emotion. Trust what comes.

7 Ask the Plant Spirit how you can honor them in your daily life. This is an act of reciprocity, essential in all relationships with the more-than-human world.

8 When the journey feels complete, offer thanks. Follow the path back the way you came, through the opening and up into the natural place where you began. Breathe deeply. When you're ready, open your eyes and return.

9 Take time to journal or draw what you experienced. The journey may continue to unfold in dreams or signs in the waking world.

Connecting with the Plants in Your Environment

When we think of "wild" places, we often picture ancient forests, an untamed jungle, or perhaps an endless desert or tundra, but any place we allow to flourish unimpeded by human hands is wild. We don't have to access "wilderness" to communicate with plants and nature. Indigenous wisdom reminds us to notice the plants growing in our midst. There are infinite worlds virtually invisible to most of us and yet they live alongside our own, surrounding us every single day—whether in backyards, meadows, the quiet green corners of neighborhood parks, and in the many forgotten places, like the plants growing up through the spaces in our well-worn sidewalks, in forgotten lots, and even in tiny window boxes.

The plants that show up repeatedly and unexpectedly in our environments are the ones we most need to work with. Over time, we might discover these are Plant Allies showing up to introduce themselves to us, inviting us into relationship. When plants appear in these special and consistent ways, they are making themselves known to us for healing and to impart teachings, insights, and inspiration. Their messages can pertain to the physical, emotional, and/or spiritual aspects of our lives. They call to the part of us still deeply connected to the natural world, inspiring a "soul remembering." The plants are "showing up" to get our attention. Even plants we view as "troublesome," such as Poison Ivy (*Toxicodendron radicans*), have a crucial place in native ecosystems and in our lives, presenting us with valuable lessons and guidance.

Everything loves to be loved and respected. When we give nature our attention, we give her our love and respect. Noticing and paying attention without judgment and with a sense of childlike curiosity is one of the best ways to begin connecting with the plants around us. When we give a plant our attention, an energetic exchange is ignited and the door to communication and understanding is cracked open. The first step is to get to know what is growing where we live, work, and frequently walk. If you have a yard, a garden, a local walking path, or a trail that you frequent, begin by noticing and identifying the plants that most stand out to you. For a longer, deeper experience, try the practice on pages 74–75.

The plants that immediately capture your attention are going to be the ones you begin to connect with first.

PRACTICE

Notice the Plants Around You

This is a wonderfully renewing exercise, which can be done in a quiet spot in your yard, a park, or a patch of earth nearby where you will not be disturbed. You could take a journal with you and write down the observations and messages you receive from the plants and nature. This exercise pairs well with the breathwork practice on page 77.

1 Stand or sit comfortably in your chosen spot. Connect with the sky around you and take a few deep and cleansing breaths. Then close your eyes and feel the ground beneath you. Imagine roots extending from your feet or seat into the Earth, anchoring you in stillness.

2 Open your eyes softly and let your gaze wander. Rather than looking for something, allow your vision to soften as your senses awaken. Let the plants come into view as if they are revealing themselves to you.

3 Notice what draws you in. Is there a particular plant you feel curious about? A leaf that catches the light, a colorful flower blooming near the path, a tiny sprout breaking through the soil, a leaf moving in the wind? Approach it slowly, as you would an old friend.

4 Take time to really see the plant—its color, its shape, its movement. What does it smell like? Is there texture? Can you hear a sound as the wind moves through it?

5 Stand or sit quietly near the plant. Place your hand close to or gently on the plant (only if you are sure it is safe to do so). Ask, without words: "Is there anything you wish to share with me today?" Let go of expectation. Simply listen with your body, your breath, your heart. Remain here for as long as you like.

6 Before you leave, offer thanks to the plant, the land, and the moment. A breath, a word, or even a simple touch of your heart is enough.

Connecting with one area regularly deepens our connections with the plants, the land, and the creatures residing there. As you continue to visit your chosen area, notice what changes depending on the day, the seasons, and the weather conditions. How do these different settings affect the plants and your perceptions? What things do you notice that you had not been aware of previously?

Shared Breath

The plants give us our very lives. They helped to create this home of planet Earth for us to live and thrive on. They provide us with food, medicine, clothing, our homes, even the very air we breathe. Without plants, humans would simply not exist. As we sit with a chosen plant, we tune into the intersection of our own cycle of respiration and that of our green friends. While we inhale oxygen and exhale carbon dioxide, plants inhale carbon dioxide and exhale oxygen. This cycle is a mirror of reciprocity between plants and humans and most creatures on Earth. Breathing with a plant is an intimate experience, as if gazing into the eyes of a beloved. In this exchange, there is no separation, only relationship. Barriers are removed, enabling us to hear the plants' voices, their songs, and the ancient wisdom they carry.

The practice on the following page shows you how to breathe with a plant. As you experience this process, an energetic exchange happens, deepening the sacred relationship and helping to ease the flow of transmissions from our plant kin. The more we practice attuning in this way, the better we receive these transmissions. Stay open to the forms these may take—as we learn to listen from the soul level, we may:

- Hear sounds like music or bells, or even words.
- Smell the scents of the plants strongly.
- Have a felt sense of the plants reaching out to us.
- Receive flashes of intuition, fleeting images, or even memories or emotions.

As we continue with this practice and the other exercises, these sensations and offerings will come to us more regularly.

PRACTICE

Breathing with a Plant

You will need to work with a live plant, which can be a wild weed, a garden plant, or even a houseplant. If you've connected with a plant in another exercise, this would be the perfect continuation of that bond.

Ask the plant's agreement before you begin. Simply send out the intention that you would like to engage with the plant in this way and pay attention to what comes back—you may hear a whispered affirmation or just a feeling that the plant would like to connect with you. Trust what you receive.

1 Sit in front of the plant—it can be placed on a table, if you like.

2 Close your eyes and engage your breath to center yourself, bringing all your attention into the present moment. Breathe into any places of tension, feeling yourself relax more with each out-breath.

3 Send your awareness out to the plant to sense its energy. Imagine the oxygen the plant is giving off as a gentle but vibrant energy, like a whisper of a tiny cloud. See yourself inhaling this energy as you breathe in and then see your out-breath as it is inhaled by the plant.

4 Feel the cycle of breathing in and out continue in an even and relaxed way, rolling like the wave on a gentle ocean. Continue for a few minutes or for as long as you like.

5 When you feel ready, gently open your eyes and send your green partner gratitude for the exchange. Take a few minutes to come completely back to the present moment.

6 Jot down any notes or impressions you experienced.

Vocal Toning

Vocal toning and chanting are ancient practices dating back thousands of years, utilized multiculturally around the world and in many spiritual and religious traditions. No doubt ancient humans were intimately aware of the rhythms inherent in nature—the rustle of leaves, the sound of the wind across open plains, the swell of the oceans, and the rush of rivers and streams.

All of nature emits frequencies that translate into sounds. Some of these are within our range of hearing, others are not. (This is easily illustrated if you've ever noticed a beloved pet reacting to sounds or vibrations that you are not aware of.) Depending on where we live, our modern lives can be fraught with sound pollution, causing stress and imbalance. We often tune common sounds out, and don't consciously register them, yet they are affecting our state of mind regardless of our level of awareness. Vocal toning and chanting can be incorporated into healing or meditation sessions to bring about inner peace, clarity, and overall well-being.

Vocal toning differs from chanting—toning involves sustaining a single syllabic sound while chanting is a word-based repetition of specific mantras, prayers, or songs from a specific culture or religious tradition. Toning produces a healing frequency that resonates down to the cellular level as it opens our depth of sensitivity and perception. Through regular practice, vocal toning helps us to connect with the unseen or unnoticed aspects of the natural world.

Toning with a plant is a simple but highly effective way to open our hearts to the energetic aspects of the plants, thereby strengthening our ability to hear their messages. It enables us to move out of our minds and focus in on our heart centers so we can receive messages directly, without our "inner critic" getting in the way. Toning with plants doesn't require any special singing talents or equipment, only an open mind and heart and a willingness to explore and deepen our connection.

PRACTICE

Vocal Toning with a Plant

You can tone with any type of live plant—a flowering or herbaceous plant, a shrub, a succulent, or even a tree! It can be a wild plant, or one in your house or garden.

The tone we will use is the "ah" tone, pronounced with a soft "a." This tone is connected to the energetic heart center, or heart chakra, located in the middle of the chest. This is a powerful tone of love and partnership, which can open lines of communication and understanding, and remove blocks.

1 Choose a plant and a quiet place where you will not be disturbed. The first time you perform this exercise, set aside at least 10–15 minutes. When you become more familiar with it, toning can be done anywhere and anytime.

2 Sit upright with your spine straight but relaxed, with the plant in front of you. If it is a small potted plant, you could place the plant on a table or even hold it in your hands.

3 Internally ask permission to connect with the plant by reaching out energetically. Use your intuition to sense the response coming back to you.

4 When you feel ready, say the "ah" tone gently and evenly, extending out the sound as long as is natural for you. Direct your toning toward the plant, pausing at the end of the tone to breathe.

5 Continue toning in an easy, comfortable way, stopping to breathe at regular, natural intervals.

6 When the exercise feels complete, pause for a few moments to enjoy the peace and stillness, and send gratitude to your Plant Ally for the connection.

7 Jot down any insights or messages you may have received.

Plant Dreaming

Many traditional Indigenous healers, medicine people, and shamanic practitioners experience the world as a dream within a dream, where nighttime dreams are considered no less valid and just as real as our "waking reality." In some instances, the dream realm is considered even more important because this is a place where we receive dialogues of the unseen, which are unfettered by our rational minds. Here, we can more easily interact with loved ones, ancestors, spirit guides, and Plant Spirits.

HOW TO ENCOURAGE PLANT DREAMING

Ideally, you should reach out to one Plant Spirit at a time, preferably one that you are already developing a relationship with. As long as it is non-poisonous (and otherwise harmless, for example to any children or pets in your household), you can place a small amount of the dried plant, wrapped in fabric or placed in a small pouch, inside your pillowcase (see page 107 for steps on how to make your own "dream pillow"). Just before you drift off to sleep, ask the Plant Spirit to visit you in your dreams.

The plants' presence can be subtle, so learning to be aware of how they present themselves is important. They could show up looking like their physical self, as a light being, a nature spirit, or they may even look humanlike. Have a pen and notebook near your bed to make notes on what you remember when you wake up.

It can take some time for plant dreaming to occur or for you to recognize it when it does, so don't be discouraged if you feel that nothing is happening right away. Most often, we get in our own way when it comes to connecting with the Plant Spirits. Remember that they want to connect with you. A preparatory ceremony can help to ease the process—see pages 82–83.

This ancient technique has been used for thousands of years by spirit workers who would receive information on the roots of illness, experience healing ceremonies, or even acquire healing or psychic abilities. The dream experienced could be of a prophetic nature, or the dream itself might be the medicine, offering up the release of grief, a soul healing, or the return of lost vitality.

For traditional herbal healers who meet Plant Spirits in the dream space, the Plant Spirit might share:

- Healing ceremonies.
- Information about the plant's healing properties.
- The ways in which the healer was meant to work with the plant.
- Information on how to harvest the plant and create medicines.

Some traditions teach that plants will not work for a herbal practitioner unless they had been introduced in some way to the Spirit of the Plant.

Dreaming with a Plant Spirit or Plant Ally is a profound and sacred practice. At times, this can happen spontaneously, drawing us across the threshold and into the dream world, where the language of plants unfolds in symbol and sensation. In the dream state, we bypass our rational minds and can receive the healing energies of the Plant Spirits directly. This is an extraordinary experience. Through reverence, intention, and consistent practice, we can create the potential to dream with a plant.

I adore when the Plant Spirits show up for me in the dream space. Plant dreams take on a different energy and feel. These are dreams I remember clearly, which no amount of time can erase. Often the plants show up quite large, echoing their prehistoric origins as I am transported to distant lands I've never visited in my waking reality. Certain plants show up large to get my attention or to make a point they don't want me to miss! Other times, they ripple with the energy of the fae realm (the liminal space where faeries, gnomes, elves, and other beings who walk in the spirit world can be found) as I see their spirit selves appearing in a multitude of different forms. Their messages come through in a variety of magical ways, which vary for each person.

PRACTICE

Plant Dreaming: A Preparatory Ceremony

To help invite a Plant Spirit into your dreams, you will need a small cup of tea made from your chosen plant, such as Mugwort (*Artemisia vulgaris*), Rose (*Rosa* species), or Chamomile (*Matricaria chamomilla*), a journal and pen, a candle or natural object (such as a stone, a feather, or a leaf), and a sprig or sachet of the plant (optional).

1 Choose a quiet place where you can sit peacefully before bed. Light a candle or hold a token from nature to help shift your awareness and anchor your focus. Dim the lights and let silence settle.

2 Take a few deep, gentle breaths. Feel your body supported by the Earth beneath you. Imagine roots extending downward, connecting you to the land, the plant kingdom, and the dream space beyond the veil.

3 Hold the cup of tea in both hands. Speak to the plant, aloud or silently: "Sacred [plant name], I welcome your spirit into my dreams tonight. If it is your will, please share your wisdom with me. I am listening."

4 Sip the tea slowly. Let the essence of the plant enter you, feeling its warmth, its taste, its energy. This is not just drinking; it is communion.

5 Close your eyes and speak your intention clearly, like a whisper through the leaves. You could say: "Show me what you wish to share," "Teach me what I'm ready to learn," or "Let me walk with you in the dreaming."

6 Blow out the candle and give thanks. If you are using it, place your sprig or sachet of the plant near or beneath your pillow. Sleep with a spirit of openness and gentle curiosity.

7 When you wake up, write down anything you remember—words, colors, feelings, symbols. Even if nothing comes, keep returning. Relationship deepens with time, and the plants dream with us on their own terms.

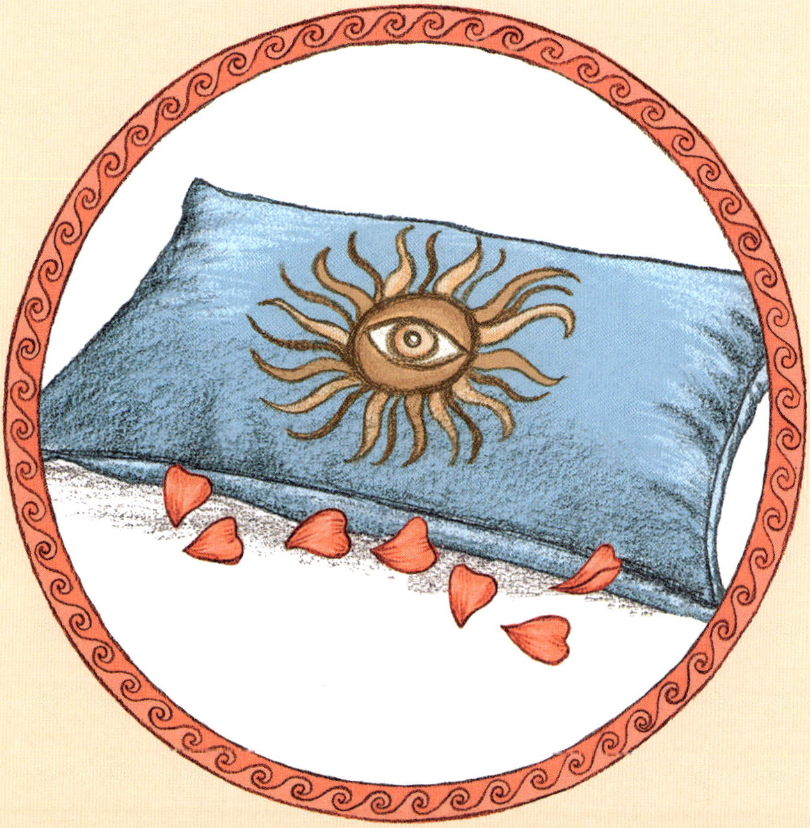

Clearing the Way for Consistent Communications

Aligning with the plants can be a joyful and transformative practice, enriching our lives in more ways than we can imagine. Having successful communications with them will take time and practice. Through teaching these methods, I've found it's common for students and even experienced practitioners to occasionally struggle to connect, at the beginning of their journey or at any point along the path. This is a natural part of the process and nothing to be concerned about.

Blocks to plant communication can arise for many different reasons, which we will explore below. There are various ways we can help to move past these blocks and restore consistent communications. It is often less about ability and more about remembering, receptivity, and unlearning what dulls our perception.

- Trying too hard: We may be too focused on trying to do the exercises "right," or have strong expectations about how the communications should come to us. Communications can come in many forms—the plants will reach out to us in a unique, personal way, which may not resemble someone else's experience. Learn to release your expectations and not put undue pressure on yourself or compare yourself to others. Honor your own experiences, holding them like the sacred treasures they are.
- Rushing: Speeding through any of the exercises or trying to cram in too much at once will result in stress and a feeling of forcing connections. When we rush, multitask, or demand answers quickly, we miss the subtle rhythms where communication takes place. Like any good relationship, the one we have with our plant friends will develop over time. Learn to savor all the moments with a relaxed state of quiet wonder and your bonds with your green allies will flourish.
- Emotional wounds, past trauma, or fear of being vulnerable: Plant Spirits often open up to us to the level of our own depth. If we're afraid of what we might find there, we may unconsciously shut down the dialogue. Building trust with a gentle Plant Spirit, such as Rose (*Rosa* species), Lemon Balm (*Melissa officinalis*), or Chamomile (*Matricaria chamomilla*), can help to create a safe space to listen again.

- **Disconnection from the Earth:** This is something that many of us have experienced for a multitude of reasons; we may have grown up in cultures that view nature as separate, silent, or inert, or we might be so connected to modern culture and a reality that does not offer space for viewing plants as sentient beings. If we've been taught that plants are "just objects" or that communication only happens with words, it can dull our ability to receive the subtle languages of the green world.

- **Lack of permission or invitation:** Plant communication is relational, not transactional. If we approach plants with an attitude of demanding or expectation rather than offering and respect, the channel may close. Honor the plants as sovereign beings and begin with a simple invitation: "I wish to listen. I welcome your presence. I honor your spirit." The plants know and respond to what is in our hearts so tuning into the space within can reopen the channels for communication.
- **Self-doubt:** The belief that we are not intuitive, not spiritual "enough," or not worthy of communication with plants can create an energetic block. But the truth is that we all come from people who spoke with plants. This is your birthright. The remembering lives in your bones. Honor and trust that.

Additional Ways to Restore Connections with the Plants

If you're still having difficulty with your communications, work through the following suggestions. These are reminders of the basic practices, along with some additional tips, which will make a monumental difference in your ability to have relationships with the plants and nature.

- Slow down: One of the most profound gateways to plant communication is simply slowing down. Sit with a plant for a while without agenda. Breathe. Notice its posture, scent, texture, and movement. Let the encounter be enough, without expecting words or signs, and without judgment. Stillness is often the first language of the green world.
- Make an offering: This act is beautiful in its simplicity and instantly fosters a connection. When we sincerely make an offering to a plant friend with love in our hearts, it is immediately known and felt by the plant. Offer something simple and sincere like a song, a strand of hair, a prayer, or a traditional offering of Tobacco (*Nicotiana* species) or Cornmeal (*Zea mays*). Offerings help reestablish reciprocity and appreciation, shifting the dynamic from "tell me" to "I honor you." When I make offerings, I thank the plant for its beauty, its presence in my life, and for the work it's doing for the Earth and other beings just by existing.
- Drum or rattle: Drumming and rattling move us out of our head space and back into our bodies, opening our feelings and intuition in the process. Both practices connect us directly with the Earth and the energetic realms where the plants live, move, and dream. Even 5–10 minutes of drumming or rattling will shift our consciousness, moving us into a state of peace and presence and back into the river of communication.
- Walk through a garden or conservatory: When we think too much, we can get in the way of the process. Casually walking through a garden or conservatory, admiring the beauty, colors, and forms of florals and botanicals, can enable us to get out of our heads and back into our senses, paving the way for our energy to circulate once again.
- Trust the subtle: Plant communication doesn't always come as a voice or vision. It may arrive as a sudden memory, a physical sensation, a mood shift in the plant's presence, a phrase that repeats in your mind, or a color or symbol that lingers. Trust what arises even if it feels quiet or uncertain.

- **Return again and again:** Relationships build over time. Revisit the same plant daily, even if only for a moment. Greet it like a friend. Write to it. Sing to it. Sit with it in different seasons. The more time spent in its presence, the more the channel opens.
- **Explore the following exercises!** The next section of this chapter explores some of the other ways we can work with the plants. This includes creating with the plants in a tangible way, either through making herbal remedies or exploring plants through arts and crafts. These practices tap into our tactile senses, enhancing our understanding of the plant world and our relationship to the plants.

Other Ways to Work with the Plants' Energies

Although the focus of this book is on communicating with the plants' energies, having their presence around us in other forms is another way to deepen our relationships. As our love of the plants grows, it's natural to want to have their vibrations around us. When we create with them through herbal remedies or art, their essences are present in those creations. Seeing a meaningful work of art or smelling the subtle fragrance of a healing herbal oil we've created with our plant friends is a delight and a reminder that they are always with us, reinforcing their lessons and gentle guidance. Having their energies surrounding us serves to strengthen the bonds we're forming with the plant and natural world.

Herbal Oils

Herbal-infused oils carry not only the physical medicine of the plant, but also its essence, its energetic imprint, and its invitation into relationship. Working with herbal oils allow us to invite the essence of a plant into our lives in a tangible, embodied way. We can incorporate herbal-infused oils before ceremony, meditation, or as simple heartfelt stand-alone rituals. When used with intention, these oils become a reinforcement and enrichment to the experiences we're having with the Green Ones.

Herbal oils can be used for many purposes: Calendula (*Calendula officinalis*) and Chamomile (*Matricaria chamomilla*) are healing to the skin; St. John's Wort (*Hypericum perforatum*) offers relief to aching muscles; and Lavender (*Lavandula* species) soothes stressed-out minds and bodies. Herbal-infused oils can also be used for spiritual or energetic purposes. For instance, an oil crafted with Mugwort leaves (*Artemisia vulgaris*) is perfect for anointing the third eye area (located in the center of the forehead) before meditation or plant communication practices.

Working with these sacred remedies can enhance plant communication, attuning us more deeply to the plant's energy, presence, and wisdom. Using the oil in preparation for ceremony helps to open the senses and align the spirit for deeper connection.

- **Breath and scent as communion:** Place a few drops of herbal oil onto your palms, rub them together, and inhale slowly. Close your eyes and feel the plant's spirit entering through the breath. Ask inwardly: "How do you wish to speak with me today? Where in my body or spirit do you wish to go?" This opens the olfactory pathways, which are deeply linked to memory, intuition, and the subconscious.

- **Anointing:** Before going about your day, place a few drops of oil onto your palms or fingertips then use these to anoint the wrists, ankles, throat, and heart area. You can use oils to strengthen an area of the body—for example, you could anoint the solar plexus chakra (the energy center located above the navel and linked to your sense of self) to help increase your self-esteem and self-confidence. You could also anoint a special object, such as a stone, a pendant, or a journal, to become your ritual companion in plant dialogue.

- **In the bath:** Add a few drops of oil to a preparatory bath before journey work, meditation, or ceremony. Mugwort or Lavender oil could be used before a dreaming ceremony; these herbs are perfect dreamtime companions and guides.
- **Oil as offering:** Offer a drop of oil to the Earth, to your altar, or to a living plant in gratitude. This completes the loop of relationship and honors the spirit of reciprocity.

PRACTICE

How to Make Herbal Oils

You can make herbal oils using fresh or dried herbs. There are two methods: cold and hot. You can use either method with fresh herbs—if you are harvesting your own, do so on a dry day, waiting until the dew has completely evaporated. This will help to keep moisture out of your remedy. You could also let the herbs wilt for 24 hours to remove excess water. If you are concerned about your oil going rancid, choose dried herbs and use the hot method to produce a more effective and concentrated oil.

Ideally, take cuttings from plants that you've grown yourself, or find an area that has an abundance of the plant. Mugwort (*Artemisia vulgaris*) grows in ample supply in many locations, for example. Use snips or garden shears to carefully cut the leaves and flowers into small pieces. Ask the plant's permission first and give thanks.

As well as the cut herbs, you will need two thoroughly clean and dry glass jars (canning jars are great), extra virgin organic olive oil, a spoon, a sieve, cheesecloth, a 4-cup/1-liter measuring cup/jug, vitamin E oil (optional), plus water, a stainless-steel double boiler and thermometer, if using the hot method.

Cold Method: Using Fresh Herbs

1. Place the cut herbs in a jar, leaving space (roughly 1 in/2.5 cm) at the top.
2. Pour in enough olive oil to completely cover the herbs.
3. Use a spoon to press the herbs down, releasing any air bubbles. You may need to add extra olive oil as the herbs absorb the oil.
4. Cap the jar tightly then place it in a sunny location. Allow the oil to sit for 4–6 weeks, shaking the jar a few times each day.

5 Line the sieve with enough cheesecloth to drape over the sides, then place the sieve over the measuring cup/jug. Pour the oil and herbs into the cloth, then gather the cloth and press gently to extract the remaining oil, allowing the oil to run through the sieve and into the measuring cup. Avoid squeezing too hard.

6 Decant the oil from the measuring cup into a fresh jar. If you like, you could let the oil sit overnight or for another couple of days after straining (to allow any additional sediment to settle to the bottom), then strain again to remove the sediment.

7 If you are using it, add the vitamin E oil (1 teaspoon per cup/240 ml of finished oil) as a preservative.

8 Store the herbal oil in the refrigerator or in a cool dark place.

Hot Method: Using Fresh or Dried Herbs

1 Place the cut herbs in the top section of a double boiler. Add enough olive oil to cover about 1 in (2.5 cm) above the herbs. Stir to completely saturate the herbs.

2 Add a few inches of water to the bottom pot of the double boiler, then place the top pot (containing the herbs and oil) on top of the bottom pot.

3 Place the double boiler on the stovetop and turn the heat on low.

4 Allow the herbal-infused oil to heat for 2–3 hours, checking it frequently for temperature (utilizing the thermometer) and stirring to avoid sticking or burning. The water should remain at an even temperature to keep the oil and herb mixture at a steady 110–115 °F (43–47 °C). Do not let the water boil.

5 Add more water to the lower pot as needed, making sure not to get any water into the oil and herbs in the top pot.

6 To finish, allow the oil to cool to room temperature then follow steps 5–8 from the cold method.

Sacred Smudge Bundles

Another way to enhance our work with our Plant Spirit friends is with smudge bundles, which are bundles of dried, aromatic herbs. They are used in a practice called smudging, whereby the bundle of herbs is burned and the resultant smoke is utilized to clear space, or ourselves, of non-beneficial energies, and to center the mind before meditation or ceremony. Smudge bundles made from a single herb can be used to invoke the Spirit of the Plant before communication practices.

Choosing and Preparing Your Herbs

Drying your own herbs for your smudge bundle will create a special connection between you and the plant(s) you are working with. Choose fresh plants that grow on a stem, such as Rosemary (*Salvia rosmarinus*), Sage (*Salvia officinalis*), Mugwort (*Artemisia vulgaris*), Lavender (*Lavandula* species), pictured below, Rose (*Rosa* species), and Pine (*Pinus* species). To ensure a long enough bundle, cut the plants low on the stem, to measure roughly 6–8 in (15–20 cm). Gather the cut herbs and hang them to dry in a warm location with good air flow. It can take from a few days up to a week for them to dry sufficiently, depending on the warmth of the room. The herbs should be dried but not crumbly.

PRACTICE

How to Make and Use a Smudge Bundle

To make and use a smudge bundle, you will need your prepared dried herbs (see page 92), twine or embroidery thread, a pair of scissors, and a heatproof bowl or dish.

1 Take a moment to center yourself. Let the plants know your purpose. Ask for permission and offer gratitude. You could say: "This bundle is being crafted for sacred use to honor your spirit and carry your medicine with respect."

2 Layer your dried herbs, placing sturdier plants, such as Rosemary or Sage, at the core and softer, more delicate ones, such as Lavender or Rose petals, toward the outside. Shape the bundle so it tapers slightly toward the base.

3 Cut a piece of twine or thread approximately 4–5 times the length of your bundle.

4 At one end of the thread, tie a knot around the base of the bundle to anchor it.

5 Wrap the thread upward in a spiral around the bundle, pulling it tight as you go. Make sure the bundle is not overly compressed to allow for airflow when burning.

6 When you get to the top, reverse the direction and spiral back down the bundle to create a crisscross pattern. Tie the thread securely at the base.

7 Hold the bundle to your heart and breathe your intention into it. You might say: "May this bundle carry the wisdom of the plants, the breath of the Earth, and the light of my purpose."

8 Light the end of the bundle over the heatproof bowl or dish, allowing the smoke to waft around yourself, a space, or an object.

9 When done, allow the bundle to extinguish itself or press the end into the bowl to put it out. Never leave the bundle burning unattended.

10 Store your smudge bundle in a clean, dry place between uses.

Flower Essences

Flowers are among the most intricate and refined expressions of the plant world. A tremendous amount of energy goes into their creation, meaning they carry the highest vibratory signature of the plant's being. Flower essences are energetic remedies that capture this subtle essence using live blooms, pure water, sunlight, and a natural preservative, such as brandy or glycerin. Unlike herbal tinctures or essential oils, flower essences do not rely on the physical constituents of the plant; they work instead with the plant's energetic imprint.

The term "flower essence" was first coined by Dr. Edward Bach, the English physician and visionary who developed Bach Flower Remedies. In the 1930s, Dr. Bach discovered 38 flower remedies, each designed to address specific emotional and mental states. His work laid the foundation for generations of flower essence practitioners to come. Since that time, many others around the world have expanded on his legacy, creating new essences from plants native to their own regions, each one carrying a unique note in the great symphony of plant healing.

These remedies interact with the subtle body, including the emotional and energetic field that surrounds us, often referred to as the auric field. Flower essences gently assist in shifting long-held emotions, thought patterns, and energetic imprints that may be contributing to imbalance or disharmony in our lives. They do not do the work for us, but they can aid in clearing away the energetic clutter, providing needed clarity and focus for change. We can work with flower essences:

- To shift out of destructive patterns of imbalance.
- To balance or heal emotional issues.
- To heal the emotional component of physical issues.
- To heal issues with others.
- To bring clarity to our relationships.
- For issues with our work or career.
- For financial issues.
- To help balance or support the chakras (the body's energy centers).
- For environmental issues.

Choosing and Working with Flower Essences

Since flower essences do not contain any of the physical aspects of the plant, they are free of side effects and will not interact with any medications or herbal remedies you may be taking. Although flower essences can be a complement to healing the energetic and emotional aspect of issues, they should never be used to replace physical or mental health treatments.

Decide which issue you would like to work on, then choose between one and five flower essences to work with. See the Resources and Further Reading section on page 141 for some resources to help you decide which flower essences to work with, depending on the issue. When you're first getting started, it is best to work with one flower essence at a time. This way, you can gauge directly how well it is working and how you react to each one. Work with the flower essence for a month, six months, or more, depending on the issue. Over time, you can build up to working with multiple flower essences at at time.

Flower essences can be placed on the body. For example, if you want to heal self-confidence issues, place a drop or two on your solar plexus chakra (the energy center located just above the navel), or place the drops on your heart chakra, in the center of your chest, if the issue is to do with love or relationships. Flower essences can also be placed on the pulse points on the wrists.

Alternatively, you can also ingest flower essences. Place 1–4 drops under the tongue three to four times a day. You can also add the drops to a glass of water then stir and sip the water throughout the day. Make sure the dropper doesn't touch either your tongue or the water. Pause for a moment of quiet after taking the essence to allow its energies to mingle with your own.

PRACTICE

Making and Storing a Flower Essence

This method of creating a flower essence utilizes a mother essence, a stock bottle, and a dosage bottle. The mother essence is used to make the stock bottle, and the stock bottle is used to make the dosage bottle, which is the one you'll use for taking the flower essence remedy. The mother and the stock are not used directly, only to make the remedy.

You will need a small glass bowl, spring water, a pair of scissors, fresh flowers (all the same type/species), three 1 oz (30 ml) amber glass dropper bottles, 80 proof brandy (which acts as a preservative), and labels—remember to label the bottles as you go, including the date, flower name, and preservative. (**Safety note:** It is your responsibility to ensure the flower is not poisonous or otherwise harmful. Seek professional advice if needed.)

It is best to make a flower essence on a sunny day. Before you begin, engage with the plant through a meditation, breathe with the plant, or connect using your intuition, and always ask the plant's permission first.

1 Fill the bowl with spring water.

2 Cut the flowers close to the base, where the blossom meets the stem, so they fall directly into the water, covering the surface.

3 Place the bowl outside in the sun for 3–8 hours.

4 Gently remove the flowers from the water, taking care to keep your fingers out of the water.

5 To make the mother essence, half-fill a dropper bottle with the flower water, topping up the other half with brandy. Cap the bottle and shake 100 times.

6 To make the stock bottle, half-fill a second dropper bottle with spring water, top up the other half with brandy, but leave a little room at the top. Add 10 drops of the mother essence, cap the bottle, and shake 100 times.

7 To make the dosage bottle, half-fill the third dropper bottle with spring water, top up the other half with brandy, again leaving a little room at the top. Add 10 drops from the stock bottle then cap the dosage bottle and shake 100 times.

Remember to only ever use the flower essence from the dosage bottle directly. Keep both the mother essence and the stock bottle so that you can continue to make more dosage bottles when you run out.

Store flower essences upright, away from light, heat, electronics, and essential oils. Flower essences remain viable for at least 10 years but with careful storage and care, they can potentially last longer. Check them periodically and get rid of any that show clouding or other signs of spoilage.

Crafting Representations of Your Plant Allies

Our Plant Allies move easily through the ethereal realms and the frequencies of imagination and art. Crafting representations of our Plant Allies is a lovely, personalized way to honor and share our affection for them. It doesn't matter if we are artistically inclined or not; what matters is what's coming from our hearts. Here are some of the artistic avenues you could explore. Whichever medium you decide to create in, allow yourself to do so with joy and wonder; there is no "right" way to do this.

Drawing

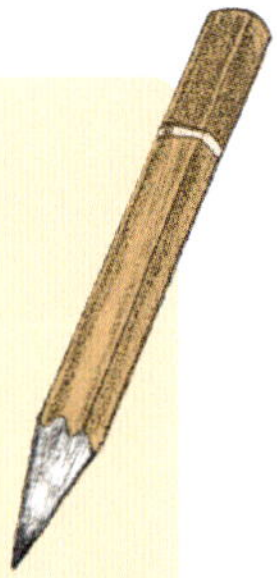

A powerful practice, drawing engages both hemispheres of the brain and invites a deep, sensory relationship with a plant. I always encourage my herbal students to draw the herbs they're learning about as a way to truly see the plant: its form, its gesture, its subtle details. Drawing becomes a bridge, a way of reaching out to the plant, creating a link that we can return to again and again. You might draw the physical plant, or maybe the Spirit of the Plant as it appears to you in a dream, meditation, or vision.

Watercolors

The fluid nature of watercolors lends itself to capturing what's subtle, shifting, or unseen, making watercolors a lovely medium for expressing the emotional or energetic essence of a Plant Spirit. Through layers of pigment and wash, you can begin to translate the feeling-tone of the plant—its mood, its movement, the way it meets you. Let go of perfection; this is about relationship, not realism.

Clay Representations

Working with clay offers a tactile and grounding way to embody your connection with a plant. As your hands shape and smooth the form, you're engaging with the Plant Spirit through touch and intention. You might sculpt a simple leaf, a seedpod, or a flower, or you might be guided to create a symbolic form that holds the plant's energy. Clay pieces can be placed on your altar, carried with you, or offered back to the Earth in ceremony. I like to keep mine on my altar as a direct connection with my Plant Allies.

Collage

Collage is a soul-mapping practice, allowing you to weave together images, textures, colors, and symbols that reflect the spirit of your Plant Ally. You could include the plant's physical form alongside representations of its medicine, its emotional tone, or its presence in your dreams.

You could begin by gathering photographs, magazine clippings, pressed leaves or petals, bits of fabric, or phrases that echo your experiences with the plant. These can live in a journal, on a vision board, or as part of an altar space. Let intuition guide your hands; this is not about aesthetics, but about invitation and insight. The collage becomes a visual altar, a reflection of your unfolding relationship with the plant.

CHAPTER 3

THE LESSONS OF SPECIFIC PLANT ALLIES

This chapter introduces you to a few of the many Plant Spirits I hold dear—those that I have cherished lifelong relationships with and others that have been pivotal to my work and teaching. As you read about each plant, imagine it imparting its medicine, wisdom, and spirit into the words, sharing a bit of history here and an anecdotal story there.

Introducing the Plant Allies

As we discussed in Chapter 1 (pages 34–37), a Plant Ally is a specific plant we have a special bond with. There are thousands of plant species in existence and I encourage you to discover the ones that resonate with you. On deciding which of my Plant Allies to include in this chapter, I focused on the ones I thought would be most accessible to people around the world in terms of direct access and ease of communication. The plants are categorized as either herbaceous plants (pages 104–127), trees (pages 128–135), or shrubs (pages 136–139), details of which are provided on the following page.

For each Plant Ally, I share a bit about their history, locality, and the ancient medicine and guidance rooted within them, and suggestions for how you can incorporate their lessons into your life. I have also provided a quote for each one. This is the plant speaking in its own voice, reaching out with words of advice, a gentle hand, a warm embrace. These words are a distillation of their spirit that you can turn to at any time to experience their essence and wisdom.

The Plant Spirits will choose to appear to each person in an incredibly unique way. All are accurate. While I may see a Plant Spirit that has a strong, female warrior presence, you may see a male presence. I may refer to a specific Plant Ally as "she" or "he," but you should address them in whatever manner feels right for you. Sometimes, the Plant Spirits appear to me as a ray of light or an energetic frequency, while at other times they look more humanlike. Other times still, they may appear more closely related to a being from the fae realm (see page 81). It all depends on what they wish to convey in that moment and which aspect of the plant's essence I'm tapping into.

Throughout the writing of this book, the plants have been very present, even peering over my shoulder, whispering their thoughts and wishes. I can tell you for certain that they cannot wait to meet you!

Herbaceous Plants

Like trees and shrubs, herbaceous plants have a vascular system for transporting water and food throughout the plant. However, they do not contain lingering woody parts. In the Northern Hemisphere, herbaceous plants will completely die back in the winter season. They are often further characterized by their life cycles, which are described as either annual (those that complete their entire life cycle in one year), biennial (those with a two-year life cycle), or perennial (those that live for more than two years).

Trees

Trees are woody, perennial plants, and some species can live for thousands of years. They typically have a single stem (often known as a trunk), which supports secondary branches. Trees and shrubs are broadly classified as either evergreen, meaning they have persistent foliage year-round, or deciduous, meaning they shed their leaves seasonally, at the end of the growing season. Given their size and presence, trees are frequently the first beings in the plant world that humans recognize. Trees hold a very special place in my heart—some of my earliest and most beloved plant friends from childhood were trees. The bond we share with the tree beings runs deep in our collective plant–human history. I have heard and witnessed countless examples of trees becoming ill or dying after the death of a human friend.

Shrubs

It can be difficult, at times, to tell the difference between a shrub and a tree. Most often, shrubs are shorter in height and have multiple stems rather than a single trunk. But just like other plants and trees, their lessons are many.

Mugwort

Artemisia vulgaris

Native to temperate Europe, Asia, and North Africa, Mugwort's range now extends through parts of North and South America, Australia, and the Philippines. Often maligned as an annoying weed, Mugwort is strong and robust, spreading easily through a process called allelopathy, in which a plant exudes a complex array of chemicals from different plant parts (through the root system in Mugwort's case) to discourage other plants from growing nearby. We can see whole swaths of Mugwort spreading in vast, unchecked rows, in part due to this process and the rapid spread of growth of her rhizomes (underground stems). As she grows wildly and with great abandon, she beckons us to embrace our wild nature, growing where we will, without apology.

Derived from the old English words *mugge* ("mug") and *wyrt* ("herb"), "Mugwort" means "the herb of the mug." This echoes back to a time when Mugwort was used for brewing sacred beers and mead before Hops (*Humulus lupulus*) became popular to brewing. Cronewort is another name for this common but otherworldly plant, speaking to her knowledge of healing and ancient wisdom like the wise crone she is.

WORKING WITH MUGWORT

Call on Mugwort when you need protection, when you seek a steady and potent ally to guide you through shadow, when you are ready to clear stagnant energy from your auric field, or awaken the energy centers of your body. Mugwort will meet you when you are prepared to step more fully into your spiritual life. We can invite Mugwort in through our intention and by keeping a dream pillow tucked under our heads as we slumber (see page 107).

Mugwort is a powerful Plant Ally, carrying tremendous ancient medicine for both the physical body and within the spiritual or energetic realms. As a bitter, Mugwort is a digestive aid, which may be one of the reasons she was originally used in brewing. She has been utilized for everything from a topical first-aid salve to heal bruising and repel insects, as a tea to bring on the menstrual cycle, and as a salve or tea to aid in sleep and to bring down a fever. In a practice known as moxibustion, dried Mugwort is burned and held close to certain points on the body to help move energy along the meridians (lines of energy traversing the length of the body) to dispel cold and dampness. As a strong energetic stimulant, Mugwort excels at moving out physical, emotional, and energetic stagnation throughout our being.

"Take my hand as I walk you through the thresholds of dreams and the world of spirit."

The Spirit of Mugwort

Mugwort's botanical name, *Artemisia vulgaris*, beckons to her association as a herb sacred to Artemis, who is the goddess of the hunt and a moon goddess of the ancient Greek pantheon, later renamed Diana by the Romans. We can see this reflected in Mugwort's physical features—the undersides of her leaves are covered in fine white hairs, which take on a silvery look especially in the moonlight.

- As a herb of the Moon, Mugwort strongly awakens our psychic vision, opening our third eye and intuitive faculties. She encourages lucid dreaming, ushering us into the way of the dreamer and engaging with our dreams as another form of plant communication and the language of the spirit. Here she can guide and protect us on our nighttime journeys, her physical teas and remedies even aiding in relaxation and inducing sleep.
- As a herb of Artemis, she is a protector of children and women, especially women during childbirth. She protects the wild forests and the wild within us. She is the one to call us back to our true selves when we feel we have lost our way and need to be reminded of who we are.

Mugwort was traditionally used in the birthing process, so it is no surprise that she is considered a threshold plant, one who walks with us through transitions, initiations, and the sacred in-between spaces of life. All plants walk between the worlds, but Mugwort holds a sacred gift for guiding us across spiritual veils into the liminal realms that shimmer just alongside ordinary reality. She sees into the dark. She perceives the unseen, the hidden, and the forgotten. She reveals what lies beneath the surface, what we may not even realize we carry. She moves out the stagnation so we can see it, too.

PRACTICE

Creating a Mugwort Dream Pillow

Made with dried herbs, dream pillows have been created for centuries to aid sleep, to safeguard the dreamer, and to inspire sweet or mystical dreams. As a guardian of the thresholds, a guide for lucid dreaming, and a protector for the dream state, Mugwort is an ideal herb for a dream pillow, but other options include Rose (*Rosa* species), Lavender (*Lavandula* species), and Hops (*Humulus lupulus*).

To make a Mugwort dream pillow, you will need two squares of fabric measuring 4 x 4 in (10 x 10 cm), thread in a matching color, a needle or sewing machine, and approximately 1 oz (30 g) of dried Mugwort herb.

1 Put the two squares of fabric together with the right sides facing inward.

2 Sew up three sides of the fabric, leaving a seam allowance of ½ in (1.3 cm).

3 Tie off the ends of your thread then turn the fabric so the right side faces out. You should now have a little pillow.

4 Stuff the pillow full of the Mugwort herb.

5 Sew up the opening, tying off the thread.

6 Place this dream pillow into your pillowcase, inviting Mugwort to travel with you on your dream journeys.

Rose

Rosa species

Can anyone look upon a Rose and not immediately be moved by her beauty and enchanting scent? I think not. And far from being just a pretty face, she is an ancient traveler and healer. According to fossil records, Rose likely originated in Central Asia more than 35 million years ago, spreading quickly along land bridges and across tectonic connections to Europe, North Africa, and North America.

Fossil records of Rose leaves and pollen have been found in China and the western United States (Colorado and Oregon), suggesting that wild Roses became established in these regions soon after migration. Climate and land connections of the time allowed Roses to diversify and adapt, eventually giving rise to the many species we know today, including *R. gallica*, *R. canina*, and *R. rugosa*. This ancient lineage makes Rose one of Earth's most enduring and widely traveled flowering plants; there are more than 150 wild species and countless varieties, estimated at more than 30,000.

Cultivation of Roses began 5,000 years ago in China, where they featured prominently in the Imperial Gardens. Traditional Chinese Medicine values Rose for her cooling and astringent nature and early healers, such as Pliny the Elder, Dioscorides, and Nicholas Culpeper, wrote of her medicinal properties. Today, Rose is employed as a tonic for the heart, to improve blood flow, to calm headaches, as an aid for sore throats, for gum health, and as a wash for skin health and beauty.

Throughout the ages, Rose has been sacred to goddesses of love, beauty, and mystery across numerous cultures. Her unfolding petals, intoxicating fragrance, and

> "I am love in all its forms. Love is the highest vibration in the Universe. The highest forms of healing are love and beauty. It is quite simple. We come into this world to create love and beauty. That is all there is."
>
> The Spirit of Rose

thorned stems speak of both vulnerability and power, making her a perfect symbol of the divine feminine in all its forms.

- In ancient Greece, Rose was beloved by Aphrodite, goddess of love and sensuality. Legends say that red Roses first sprang from the Earth where Aphrodite's tears mingled with the blood of her beloved Adonis.
- To the Romans, Rose became sacred to the goddess Venus, embodying passion and allure.
- In ancient Egypt, Rose was associated with the goddess Isis, the great mother and healer, representing resurrection and eternal love.
- In Sufi mysticism, Rose is the symbol of divine love, her scent drawing the soul toward union with the Beloved.
- Even in Christian mysticism, Rose became a symbol of Mary, the "Mystical Rose," whose compassion and grace mirror the soft yet unwavering spirit of the flower.

Across time and tradition, Rose has remained a universal emblem of the heart, healing emotional wounds, opening pathways to intimacy, and reminding us that true beauty holds both softness and strength.

WORKING WITH ROSE

Call on Rose when you are in need of more love, whether that be self-love or the love of someone special. If you need to find your *joie de vivre*—joy of life—and passion once again, Rose will not disappoint. Rose also aids in healing from heartbreak and grief or when you feel that life has let you down. Try the meditation on page 110 whenever you need a dose of Rose's loving energy.

PRACTICE

Rose Blossom Meditation

This meditation will surround you in the essence of Rose, which feels like being encapsulated in a safe, warm cocoon.

1 Close your eyes and take a slow, gentle breath.

2 Imagine a single Rose of any color that calls to your heart. See it in your mind's eye: soft petals, vibrant center, quiet radiance.

3 With each breath you take, the Rose begins to grow, expanding gently and gracefully until it becomes as large as your body, then larger still.

4 Now, you are inside the Rose, held within her spiral of petals, bathed in her sweet fragrance, surrounded by her warmth. Let the energy of Rose envelop you—it is soft, wise, protective, and loving. Breathe it in. Let it infuse your heart, your cells, your spirit, feeling your energy renewed and cleansed.

5 Stay here for a few quiet moments, receiving whatever messages or sensations arise.

6 When you feel ready, offer your gratitude to Rose, and slowly begin to return to the present space, carrying her essence with you.

St. Joan's Wort

Hypericum perforatum

Widely known as St. John's Wort, I most often call this plant St. Joan's Wort. From the first time she appeared to me in her spirit form, she looked very much like St. Joan of Arc—she was shining, radiant, and filled with Light that nearly blinded me. St. Joan, like the plant herself, represents courage, illumination, and resilience in the face of darkness. This shift in naming reflects the deeper energetic and symbolic relationship that a number of healers feel with this powerful Plant Spirit.

St. Joan's Wort challenges the preconceived notions we have about her. Her physical medicine is usually connected with helping to heal depression. Although she has been utilized frequently for this purpose, her other attributes are considerable. Many herbalists, myself included, work with this herb topically to heal wounds—she shines at healing deep cuts, burns, bruises, sunburn, nerve pain, and topical rashes.

Native to Europe, North Africa, and Western Asia she is now found throughout the temperate regions of the world including the United States and Canada. For centuries, St. Joan's Wort has been revered as a powerful spiritual protector. In ancient Greece, she was used to ward off illness, curses, and unwanted spirits, earning the name *fuga daemonium*, or "demon chaser." Worn, carried, or hung over doorways, the plant was believed to shield against dark forces and misfortune. Her golden blooms, aligned with the Summer Solstice, were gathered for midsummer rituals and folk traditions across Europe—sprigs were placed under pillows for psychic protection, pressed into books for safekeeping, or woven into midsummer wreaths to invite blessings and dispel fear. Long associated with Light, courage, and truth, St. Joan's Wort continues to serve as a spiritual ally, offering clarity, energetic cleansing, and protection on the soul's path.

In her Plant Spirit form, St. Joan's Wort enables us to ignite the warrior within. Through my work with her, I have seen her presence as a true warrior who comes from a place of quiet strength rather than loud egoic force (which is not strength at all but weakness). She gathers the Light within, concentrating it and sending it to us when we most need it.

"I will shine my Light until you can find your own. I will be your strength and your shield, carrying you safely through the darkness."

The Spirit of St. Joan's Wort

WORKING WITH ST. JOAN'S WORT

Call on St. Joan's Wort when you need protection, when you cannot seem to find your inner Light, or when you are struggling to stand in your truth. She is a spirit protector, especially when those around you are trying to diminish your Light. She is a heart protector, filling us with the courage to simply be who we are, regardless of who others may think we are. If she is our ally, she will faithfully stand by us, offering courage, strength, clarity, and the ability to see the truth. Invite her energy in by making and working with an infused oil (see opposite).

PRACTICE

Making and Using a St. Joan's Wort Oil

Nothing is quite as mesmerizing as the mystical process of making a St. Joan's Wort infused oil. Although the flowers are clearly yellow in color, a potent, infused oil will transform into a deep, rich red, due to the presence of hypericin (a naturally occurring red-colored compound) and its derivatives in the plant, which are also responsible for many of its medicinal properties.

You will need to work with fresh plant material to make the oil, following the instructions on pages 90–91. Fortunately, St. Joan's Wort is found on every continent except for Antarctica, flowering very close to the Summer Solstice—19–22 June in the Northern Hemisphere, or 21 or 22 December in the Southern Hemisphere. Depending on the weather, she can continue to bloom for a few weeks and up to a couple of months. Look for her in bright sunny locations that receive at least 6–8 hours of full sun a day. She can adapt to many different soil types but prefers well-drained, moist conditions.

Place a few drops of the oil in the palms of your hands and inhale deeply as you embrace the scent and essence of St. Joan's Wort. The oil can also be:

- Massaged onto sore muscles and bruises.
- Placed over your heart for courage or over your solar plexus (upper abdomen) when you need quiet confidence and strength.
- Used anywhere on the body or in the home to bring the energy, strength, protection, and vitality of St. Joan's Wort wherever needed or desired.

Jewelweed

Impatiens capensis

Spend time watching rain droplets on Jewelweed and you will quickly understand this plant's most common namesake. The water beads up, appearing as bright, mesmerizing liquid jewels. The effect is breathtaking, especially in the early morning light. A beloved wild companion in North American wetlands, Jewelweed appears in late summer with glowing orange or yellow pendant-like blooms, growing in abundance in areas with good water sources, often along swamps, near areas of standing water, or by slow-moving streams.

Jewelweed has long been honored by Indigenous peoples of North America as gentle medicine for skin eruptions, Nettle (*Urtica dioica*) stings, fungal infections, and insect bites. The Mohegan have been known to use the plant as a burn ointment and apply the crushed flower buds to cuts and bruises, while the Ojibwe spread the plant's fresh juice on the head for headache relief. When her leaves are pressed, her fresh sap becomes a soothing balm, easing the itch from irritating skin rashes caused by urushiol,

"I come where the waters gather, where emotion and earth meet. I am the balm for the sting, the ease after resistance. Let me teach you the grace of softening—how to let go, to grow in shadows, and to receive the abundance that flows when you no longer grip so tightly, reminding you that what is meant for you will return with gentleness and joy."

The Spirit of Jewelweed

an oily chemical found in plants such as Poison Ivy (*Toxicodendron radicans*), Poison Sumac (*T. vernix*), and Poison Oak (*T. diversilobum*). Poultices (mashed-up plant material applied topically) of Jewelweed are used on bruises, eczema, skin rashes, and burns.

Much to the delight of children and the young at heart, Jewelweed's exploding seed pods have earned her another common name of Touch-Me-Not. Jewelweed plants herself with joyous abundance, her seeds spread widely, and her blooms return and multiply without strain, embodying the promise of effortless renewal. She holds the space for softening, for release, and for healing. Her energetic medicine is water-like; cool, calming, and deeply merciful toward bodies and hearts in discomfort.

WORKING WITH JEWELWEED

Call on Jewelweed when you need to connect with the abundance in your life and spirit, when you need to assert your boundaries firmly but gently, or when you need soothing for places of irritation. Her medicine aids us in returning to a state of flow, teaching us to release when needed, protect what's tender, and soften into peace.

A wonderful way to work with Jewelweed is with her flower essence (see pages 94–97), which can be utilized when you need to soothe and calm irritated emotions, restore creative flow, and connect with the abundance in your life. You could make your own following the steps on pages 96–97, if you have plants growing nearby; if not, purchase a good-quality flower essence. A Jewelweed essence can be called on to strengthen and support the sacral chakra (the energy center located in the lower abdomen below the navel) to help balance the emotions while maintaining a sense of rootedness and centeredness.

Lavender

Lavandula species

Native to the dry, rocky landscapes of the Mediterranean, Middle East, and parts of India, Lavender is a beloved garden plant that is grown in abundance in areas around the world (most notably in Provence, France) for her precious volatile oils. While there are 47 naturally occurring species, over 450 hybrid varieties of hybrids have been created given the popularity of this fragrant bloom. Her lovely scent is much of where her magic comes from. I can scarcely even think of Lavender without taking a deep inhalation and feeling an unmistakable sense of relaxation. Her scent is a medicine unto itself, bypassing the brain's higher centers of reason, immediately calming our nervous system.

Lavender has long been utilized by humanity to relax, to heal burns, to calm bug bites, and to ease anxiety. Her oils contain antiseptic and skin-rejuvenating properties, making her an excellent addition to herbal first-aid salves and remedies. Symbolizing purity, devotion, serenity, and calm, Lavender has also been used throughout history to ward off evil, cleanse spaces, and invite clarity of spirit.

- Deriving its name from the Latin word *lavare*, meaning "to wash," Lavender was prized by the ancient Greeks and Romans, being used in baths, hair rinses, and laundry for its cleansing scent and association with cleanliness.
- The Greek physician Dioscorides described Lavender as a remedy for headaches, indigestion, sore throats, and wound-healing.

"I carry peace in the midst of the storm. Where tempests rage, I bring stillness. Where the mind spins, I soothe the breath. I settle the heart like twilight settles the sky—softly, surely, without demand. Let me wrap you in calm and remind you that serenity is your birthright."

The Spirit of Lavender

- In medieval and Renaissance magic, Lavender was placed in dream pillows, sachets, or altar bundles for love, sleep, protection, and spiritual balance.
- In medieval Europe and onward through to the 1800s, it was a common practice to "strew" Lavender flowers on floors inside homes for their disinfectant properties, to keep pests away, and for the calming scent.
- Nicholas Culpeper, a seventeenth-century herbalist, noted Lavender as a "mercurial herb" that both steadied the mind and repelled negative energies.
- Today, Lavender is widely used in aromatherapy and flower essence practices to invite peace, open the heart, and support energetic alignment, not just physically but emotionally and spiritually.

Lavender is one of my favorite Plant Spirits to journey with—this always feels like a "mini vacation" where I find myself in a more perfect state of calm, focused completely in the moment. She helps me to clear away the "unnecessary" and focus on what is good and beautiful in the moment. As a guardian of the heart and spirit, she invites calm into chaos, clarity into confusion, and kindness toward the self. Her energy is a gentle purifier that softens wounds, reveals our connection to higher vibration, and opens us to divine insight.

WORKING WITH LAVENDER

Call on Lavender when you need a strong dose of calm and help maintaining your sense of inner peace despite what is going on around you. She helps to dispel negative energies and invite in the strong and protective presence of love and serenity, providing a soothing hand to remind us that "all will be well." Lavender connects us to our crown chakra (the energy center located slightly above the top of the head)—our connection to divinity. Invite Lavender in through her smoke by creating a smudge bundle (see pages 92–93), using Lavender alone or with other plants.

Dandelion

Taraxacum officinale

Few plants are more resilient, tenacious, and generous than the humble Dandelion. She is a symbol of hope, ever reminding and encouraging us to not give up. This sunny little plant naturalizes easily and can be found on every continent except Antarctica. Refusing to be subdued, she grows up through cracks in sidewalks, along driveways, and in the middle of lawns, if you are lucky! I have a serious case of "Dandelion envy" when I see lawns covered in these radiant yellow mini-Suns. Dandelion is another of my earliest Plant Allies—I have a photograph of myself as a child intently staring at a Dandelion flower, completely mesmerized. I often picked Dandelions for my mother and happily blew their seeds everywhere, hearing their joyous laughter on the wind.

Dandelion has long been valued as both a food and a medicine—every single part of this herb has been used for both. The flowers are often made into fritters, baked into breads, or tossed into salads; the leaves are used for bitter salad greens; and the roots can be roasted and made into a healthful coffee substitute.

WORKING WITH DANDELION

Call on the sunny power of Dandelion when you need healing from long-held sadness and grief, to release toxicity, or to strengthen your solar plexus chakra (the energy center located in the upper abdomen) to boost your confidence and self-esteem. Dandelion brings rays of happiness shining brightly, helping us to find joy all around us in nature and in our everyday lives.

I love creating art with Dandelion. You can invite her joyful energy into your life through drawing, watercolor, collage, or any other creative activity you enjoy (see pages 98–99).

As a herbalist, I work with Dandelion frequently. Like her seeds, which can travel upward of 63 miles (100 km), her healing properties are loved around the world. She can aid in healing all sorts of human maladies—she can bring cleansing and nourishment to the kidneys and liver, support digestion and the immune system, and aid in balancing blood sugar levels. Infused oils of Dandelion can assist the body in releasing pent-up tension and emotion.

As with many of the plants in this book, Dandelion's journey began many millennia ago (around 30 million years ago, to be exact), and healers and herbalists have been working with Dandelion for more than a thousand years.

- Fossil records indicate Dandelion originated in Eurasia and spread rapidly, given its ease of reproduction thanks in part to its lightweight, parachute-like seeds and regenerative taproots.
- Arabian physicians were healing with Dandelion in the tenth and eleventh centuries, as was also being done in India.
- In the sixteenth and seventeenth centuries, English herbalists John Gerard and Nicholas Culpeper worked with her to heal the liver and spleen and to aid weak digestion.
- Her journey continued to North America in the early 1600s as a transplant to the early colonies having traveled aboard the *Mayflower* ship. Here, her medicine was quickly adopted by Indigenous peoples who worked with her to calm the body, ease pain, and purify the blood.
- Traditional Chinese Medicine works with another species of Dandelion, *T. mongolicum*, to treat infections.

Dandelion is symbolic of the astrological sign Leo, in part thanks to her association with the Sun but also due to her French namesake *dent de lion*, meaning "tooth of the Lion," given the coarse, toothlike edges of her leaves.

"I am one with the Infinite Sun, rooted in strength, carried by the wind, and glowing with the Sun's eternal joy."

The Spirit of Dandelion

Burdock

Arctium lappa

Burdock is one of the toughest plants I know. I jokingly tell my students that engaging with Burdock is not a quick dalliance, but a long-term relationship. It's true! Burdock's work is far-reaching, and it requires commitment whether we are healing the physical body, the emotions, or the energy bodies.

An ancient healer originating in Europe and Asia, now naturalized across North America and New Zealand, Burdock is so respected by many an Indigenous medicine person that they will work nearly exclusively with this one plant; this is how involved she is with so many body systems. Burdock's healing capabilities are felt in the liver, the blood, the digestive system, the lymphatic system, the urinary system, the immune system, and even the endocrine system. Her medicine is complex and boundless.

She works the same way with emotions and our energy systems as she does with our bodies, pulling out all the "gunk." Growing in some of the most difficult and rockiest soils, Burdock tunnels downward to unearth what we have stuffed and hidden

WORKING WITH BURDOCK

Call on Burdock when you are ready to do the heavy lifting and to make necessary changes—when you need a strong hand while traveling into what you have repressed and locked away. Burdock has an impeccable sense of timing, bringing it all up at a pace we can manage. She is equally protective and simultaneously nurturing and nourishing—the tough teacher we didn't know we needed but are so glad to have in our lives. If you are so fortunate as to ally with this plant, plan on a long-term relationship. Try the meditation on page 123 to experience the grounding strength of Burdock.

"I dig deep to unearth the hidden and the forgotten, bringing it to the Light for healing. I anchor you to the innermost sacred places where truth lives, where strength grows unseen. I clear the heaviness from your path, wrap you in my quiet protection, and remind you that nourishment begins at the root."

The Spirit of Burdock

away, pulling it out into the Light for clearing and releasing. It is not the prettiest of inner work, but it is necessary, life-saving work. While she is approachable, she is also serious. She will dig up the things you want to ignore and forget about. She roots out the things that stay in shadow—the things that will harm us the most—forcing us to deal with them. In the same breath, she is detoxifying and clearing, nourishing and gentle, providing support where required.

Energetically, Burdock is stellar at supporting the root chakra (the energy center located at the base of the spine) and the earth star chakra (located outside of the physical body, roughly 12 in/30 cm below the feet), strengthening our connection with the Earth, providing protection, and releasing toxic, long-held emotions such as anger, bitterness, and resentment. Burdock's lessons are many and very personal as she quickly gets to the "root" of any issue.

My relationship with Burdock has always been an intense one. From the moment I met this plant, I voraciously searched her out, continually planting the seeds to always be sure to have ample supply of her fresh roots, leaves, flowers, and seeds. As a young herbalist and wild forager, I scouted the places where the earth was recently disturbed to find Burdock hard at work.

As she is healing for humans, Burdock is also healing to the Earth, breaking up compacted dirt, bringing nutrients to the surface, and preventing soil erosion. She provides food for pollinators, such as Painted Lady Butterflies (*Vanessa cardui*) and Ghost Moths (*Hepialus humuli*), and for other beings such as Ring-Necked Pheasants (*Phasianus colchicus*) and American Goldfinches (*Spinus tristis*).

In folk and magical traditions across Europe and North America, Burdock has been used for protection, purification, and attracting abundance. Her roots were placed around homes or worn as amulets for shielding against curses or negative influences.

PRACTICE

Burdock Grounding Meditation

Utilize this meditation whenever you are feeling ungrounded, scattered, confused, or disconnected from yourself and the Earth. It will have a strong grounding effect on your mind and body, allowing you to become rooted in the Earth, feeling calm and centered.

1. Find somewhere, indoors or outdoors, to sit comfortably, either with your feet flat on the floor or cross-legged.
2. Close your eyes and take a slow, deep breath in and out, then another, letting each exhale draw you further into stillness.
3. Imagine Burdock growing before you, her tall, broad leaves catching the light, her sturdy stem rising from the soil. See her deep taproot sinking far below the surface, winding into the rich, dark earth.
4. With your next exhale, imagine your own roots extending down from the soles of your feet or the base of your spine, weaving into the earth alongside Burdock's. Feel the stability, the weight, the unshakable connection to the land.
5. Breathe in her strength. Breathe out any heaviness, tension, or scattered thoughts, letting them flow down into the soil where they are transformed.
6. Hear her voice in the stillness: "Root yourself here. The Earth will hold you. You are safe to stand strong." Pause here for as long as you like.
7. When you're ready, draw your awareness slowly back to your body, feeling supported, steady, and renewed. Carry Burdock's grounded protection with you as you move through your day.

Daisy

Leucanthemum vulgare

Native to Europe and western Asia, Daisy is now also found throughout North and South America, Australia, and New Zealand. Depending on where you live, Daisies bloom at the end of May through June and are often found in fields and border areas. One can't help but be uplifted by the sight of Daisy flowers gently swaying in the shining sun. Sacred to the Greek goddess Artemis, the energy of Daisy is one of joy in the simplest and purest things of life, especially those found in nature. Like Artemis, Daisy is a protector of wild places, animals, plants, and people.

Although Daisy is not often thought of as having medicinal uses, this lovely perennial has been used for centuries by Native American peoples as a spring tonic, an eye wash, and as fever medicine. Nicholas Culpeper, a seventeenth-

"No matter how great or small, everything in this Universe has its own place in the Divine Heart and its own expression of Divine Light. Let yours shine forth no matter where you find yourself."

The Spirit of Daisy

century English physician, botanist, and astrologer, recommended Daisy for healing wounds, both internal and external. Daisy is known to have antispasmodic (spasm-relieving), diuretic (urine-inducing), and fever-reducing properties and can be made into a spring tea.

Daisies hold a special place in my heart. One of the first plants I learned to identify, as a young child I spent countless hours marveling at the sight of their blossoms dancing in the breeze, their every movement filled with childlike joy and exuberance. I appreciate Daisy's symbolism of innocence, purity, and simplicity—not just innocence but innocent perception. The kind of perception steeped in the lightness of non-judgment in which we allow our observational experiences to unfold without preconception. This is the place at which we are open and teachable (not unlike Buddhism's concept of having a "beginner's mind"), approaching each situation with a sense of newness. Daisy reminds us to reconnect with the "innocent perception" we had as children, when the world was still magical and filled with wonder. Because it still is. It only requires a shift in your perception, and new worlds will open up.

WORKING WITH DAISY

Call on Daisy when you feel spacey or ungrounded, when you need to reset your priorities, or when you are feeling disconnected from Mother Earth and your higher self. You can invite Daisy into your life simply by spending time in the presence of these flowers and meditating on their energy. Even gazing at photographs of Daisies will bring in their properties of childlike joy, wonder, focus, and protection.

Ice Plant

Diphylleia grayi

My relationship with Ice Plant began when he showed up for me in an especially intense and meaningful shamanic journey (see pages 62–71). At the time, I had never seen the plant before. He conveyed his name as "Ice Plant" and shared details about the natural habitat in which he grows. After some research, I was able to find photographs of this rare plant. Over time, I've found his online presence growing as more people become interested in this stunning botanical treasure.

Ice Plant, also called the Skeleton Flower or Ghost Flower, is native to the cool, moist mountain forests of northern and central Japan (Honshu and Hokkaido), parts of Sakhalin, and the highlands of China. Like his close relative Mayapple (*Podophyllum peltatum*), he flourishes in shaded understories (the layer of plants growing below the main forest canopy) with nutrient-rich soil and consistently high humidity, thriving only in temperate woodlands with dappled light, and rarely tolerating heat or dryness.

WORKING WITH ICE PLANT

Call on Ice Plant when you seek clarity in the midst of confusion and the courage to reveal your inner shining self. He is an ally in moments of transformation, aiding in the release of the stories we carry, enabling us to embrace our vulnerability and stand vibrantly in the beauty of our authenticity.

Ice Plant reminds us that transparency is not weakness, but a luminous strength that allows the soul's intricate beauty to be seen. Invite his energy in through meditation or the shamanic journey when you wish to see through illusion, uncover hidden truths, or move gracefully through emotional storms.

This rare perennial beholds an enchanted vision seldom seen in nature: petals that turn crystal clear when wet, revealing their delicate, lacelike veining before returning to opaque white as they dry. This transformation is due to a unique cellular structure—when dry, air pockets scatter light through the petals and when rain fills these spaces, light passes straight through, rendering the petals transparent, like glass or ice. From May through July, these ethereal blossoms unfurl, later giving way to clusters of striking cobalt blue berries that glow against the broad green leaves through late summer.

In the realm of metaphysical properties, Ice Plant is a living symbol of transformation, clarity, and truth revealed under pressure. He teaches that vulnerability can be beautiful, and that moments of change, like petals in the rain, can strip away illusion to reveal our authentic self. His energy supports emotional transparency, release of hidden truths, and embracing one's inner Light even in shadowed or challenging times. He is a gentle ally for self-discovery, resilience, and seeing the beauty in impermanence.

"Let the rain come. Let it soften you into something more real. What appears delicate is simply becoming clear and what you reveal in the quiet is the most sacred part of you."

The Spirit of Ice Plant

Elder

Sambucus nigra

Growing abundantly across Europe, southwestern Asia, and northern Africa, this species of Elder has naturalized in North America alongside native *Sambucus* species. Elder is a plant my grandfather healed with and spoke of fondly. Unfortunately, I never met him, but I feel a connection to him through creating herbal remedies and engaging with the spirit of this incredible Plant Ally. True to form, Elder fosters connections to our ancestors, and why wouldn't she? Many of our descendants have adored this plant, often describing her as the "medicine chest of the people." She has been honored as a healing plant throughout countless generations and cultures.

- In ancient Greece and Rome, the flowers, berries, bark, and leaves were used to ease respiratory illness, soothe fever, and support digestion.
- Medieval texts document Elder being used in teas, syrups, vinegars, and wines to prepare people for plague conditions.
- German physician Martin Blochwich wrote *The Anatomy of the Elder* in the 1630s, detailing recipes for using this plant to treat everything from coughs and fevers to wounds and digestive issues.
- In North America, Indigenous peoples used *S. canadensis*, a related species, for fevers, colds, coughs, digestive upset, and for blood-purifying and strengthening tonics. The bark was decocted and used topically for pain and swellings of the legs.
- Today, Elder flowers and berries continue to be used and studied for their anti-inflammatory, antioxidant, diaphoretic (sweat-inducing), diuretic (urine-inducing) and immune-supportive effects, and relief from colds, sinusitis, and mild fevers.

"Stand within my circle and no harm shall reach you. I am the threshold and the watchful eye, the root in this world and the branch in the next. Under my protection, you may walk between worlds and return with your spirit whole."

The Spirit of Elder

My beloved Grandmother Elder, as I call her, is steeped in folkloric mystery. Across European legends, Elder is sacred to a spirit called the Elder Mother, who presides over protection, healing, and the boundary between worlds. Folk tradition held that one must chant or request permission before cutting an Elder tree. Being connected to transformation and dream portals, sleeping beneath an Elder tree was believed to invite vivid dreams, especially of faery realms. In fairy-lore, the plant's wood was often fashioned into simple musical instruments, tying Elder to spirit song and communication with the faery realm.

WORKING WITH ELDER

Call on Grandmother Elder when you are at a crossroads in your life and need safe passage between what is no longer and what is not yet—when you feel depleted in body, heart, or spirit, and need renewal from the inside out. Invite her spirit when you wish to strengthen your connection to ancestral wisdom, deepen your dreams, or walk with confidence between the seen and unseen worlds. She wraps you in protection while awakening your inner radiance, guiding you to live from a place of wholeness.

Invite Elder in by sitting in her presence. Notice the scent of her flowers in spring or the dark weight of her berries in late summer. Let your senses absorb her energy—the balance of both light and shadow, protection and healing. It is a loving gesture to bring an offering to your visit. See page 47 for ideas on what to bring her.

Eucalyptus

Eucalyptus species

Eucalyptus is native to Australia and nearby islands, where it has shaped the landscape, ecology, and culture for over 50 million years. With more than 700 species, Eucalyptus thrives in diverse habitats, from coastal plains to mountain ranges, and is one of the tallest flowering plants on Earth. Its aromatic leaves contain powerful essential oils that protect the tree from pests and reduce competition from other plants.

For many Aboriginal peoples of Australia, Eucalyptus was and remains a respected medicine tree. The leaves were used as poultices (mashed-up plant material applied topically) for wounds and fevers, and the vapors were inhaled for clearing respiratory congestion. Modern herbalism and aromatherapy recognize Eucalyptus oil for its antimicrobial, decongestant, and anti-inflammatory qualities, making it a beloved ally for colds, coughs, and sinus health. Its scent clears the head and deepens the breath, reminding the body to release what it no longer needs.

WORKING WITH EUCALYPTUS

Call on Eucalyptus when you need to clear away heaviness, confusion, or the lingering "fog" of illness or grief. She is a strong ally for renewal, opening the breath, expanding the mind, and protecting the heart. Turn to her when you are ready to let go of what clings to you, to cleanse your energy field, and to breathe deeply into the present moment. Invite Eucalyptus into your life through the sacred pathways of scent and breath. Inhale her essential oil or the aroma of her fresh or dried leaves, and feel her clarifying, protective energy wash over you.

Eucalyptus is a plant of clearing, renewal, and protection. Energetically, she sweeps away stagnant energies, emotional heaviness, and mental fog, replacing them with a sense of spacious clarity. In Plant Spirit work, she is a guardian of the breath, helping us release grief, open our lungs to life, and invite fresh perspective. She carries the energy of both cleansing and resilience, grounding us even as she expands our awareness.

Perhaps no creature embodies Eucalyptus more than the Koala (*Phascolarctos cinereus*). These gentle marsupials live high among Eucalyptus branches, their diet formed almost exclusively from the leaves of certain species. The Eucalyptus provides them not only with food, but with shelter and safety from predators. In turn, Koalas remind us of the deep and sacred interdependence between plant and animal, teacher and student, the rooted and the roaming. Eucalyptus holds Koalas as kin, just as she may hold us when we rest in her protective energy.

"Breathe, child. I will sweep the fog from your mind, clear the weight from your chest, and wrap you in the clean air of beginnings. With me, you can let go and fill yourself with life again."

The Spirit of Eucalyptus

Sugar Maple

Acer saccharum

One of my earliest Plant Allies was Sugar Maple—a most loved tree of my childhood home that I would sit in for hours (see page 38). Sugar Maple is native to eastern and central North America, thriving in cool climates with rich, well-drained soil. It is a long-lived tree, often reaching 300 years or more, and is famed for its spectacular autumn foliage of gold, orange, and red.

While most celebrated for its sap boiled down into maple syrup, Sugar Maple has also been used medicinally. Indigenous peoples of North America, including the Anishinaabe and Haudenosaunee, tapped the trees for the sap (by creating a hole in the trunk), using it not only for food but as a tonic for kidney health, as a springtime source of minerals, and for balancing the body after winter's scarcity. Inner bark infusions have sometimes been used for coughs or digestive complaints.

Sugar Maple embodies balance, generosity, and grounded vitality. She offers nourishment while teaching patience as her sweet sap only flows after the cold

WORKING WITH SUGAR MAPLE

Call on Sugar Maple when you need to replenish your reserves, cultivate patience, or remember the joy of giving and receiving. She helps you stand tall in your own strength while offering your gifts generously to the world.

Invite Sugar Maple into your life by sitting beneath her limbs with your back supported by her trunk. Feel her steadying presence and breathe in her sweet, loving energy.

of winter, illustrating how abundance often follows stillness. She is a guardian of inner resources, reminding us that true self-care is a necessity, not a luxury. She reconnects us to the energy of the Divine Mother, embracing us as only a mother can, strengthening our connection to the Earth. She guides us in making peace with and loving our bodies as we love hers. Sugar Maple encourages steady growth, emotional resilience, and the joy of sharing one's gifts with others.

To the First Nations of her homeland, Sugar Maple was a gift from Creator, offering both sustenance and a signal of seasonal change. Maple sugaring became a springtime ceremony and a communal event, marking renewal and the return of life's sweetness.

"I hold the sweetness of life in my veins, and the strength of centuries in my roots. Stand with me, and you will remember patience ripens every gift worth giving."

The Spirit of Sugar Maple

Sassafras

Sassafras albidum

Native to eastern North America, ranging from the Great Lakes to Florida and as far west as Texas, Sassafras is recognizable by its three distinct leaf shapes on the same tree (unlobed, mitten-shaped two-lobed, and three-lobed). A small to medium deciduous tree that prefers sunny edges and well-drained soil, its aromatic roots, bark, and leaves carry a warm, spicy-sweet scent that lingers in memory.

For countless generations, Indigenous peoples of North America, including the Cherokee, Choctaw, and Creek, have turned to Sassafras for both food and medicine. Decoctions of the root bark have been used to treat fevers, rheumatism (conditions affecting the joints and connective tissue), and skin conditions, while teas have been brewed for cleansing the blood and supporting digestion. Sassafras leaves are used in Creole cooking as filé powder, a thickener and seasoning for gumbo—a thick, savory stew or soup originating from Louisiana, USA.

WORKING WITH SASSAFRAS

Call on Sassafras when you need to reawaken your energy and sense of purpose. She is an ally for fresh starts, for journeys into the unknown, and for reconnecting with the warmth of your own vitality. Seek her out when you need both grounding in your roots and the courage to follow new paths. Invite in the energy of Sassafras by holding a Sassafras leaf or sitting quietly near her. Breathe in her spicy, uplifting scent and allow her energy to stir your spirit, noticing what feelings or visions arise in you.

Modern herbalism recognizes Sassafras for its diaphoretic (sweat-inducing), carminative (digestive-soothing), and mild anti-inflammatory properties. However, because safrole, a compound in Sassafras oil, has been linked to toxicity in high doses, contemporary use is generally limited to short-term, low-dose preparations, and to culinary applications of the dried leaves.

Sassafras is a plant of renewal, vitality, and adaptability. Energetically, she is a root-and-branch connector, linking us to our ancestral lineage while supporting forward movement into new chapters of life. She brings warmth to the spirit, stirs inspiration, and awakens curiosity. Sassafras holds deep roots in Native American culture, respected not only for its healing uses, but also as a trade item and a seasonal marker, its fragrant roots dug up in spring or fall, its bright green summer leaves becoming yellow in the fall, signaling the turn of the year. I was first introduced to Sassafras while attending a powwow (a gathering of Indigenous peoples of North America involving singing, dancing, and traditional foods and drinks) with my dad. Sassafras is served as a traditional tea early in the year for celebration and physical cleansing. This is a wonderful tradition I honor every spring. (**Safety note:** It is advisable to seek professional advice if you intend to ingest Sassafras in any form.)

"I am the warm wind that stirs your spirit, the scent that calls you home, and the spark that urges you forward. Root yourself in the wisdom of where you've been, and step boldly onto the road that awaits."

The Spirit of Sassafras

Spicebush

Lindera benzoin

Close cousin to Sassafras (see pages 134–135), Spicebush is also in the Lauraceae (Laurel) family and is native to eastern North America, thriving in moist woodlands, along stream edges, and in shady thickets. In early spring, before the forest leafs out, she brightens the understory with clusters of tiny yellow blossoms that perfume the air with a subtle spice. These lovely, vibrant flowers are an exciting signal for me every spring of the coming season of warmth and sun.

Used traditionally by Indigenous peoples of North America, including the Cherokee, for colds, fevers, and digestive complaints, Spicebush's aromatic leaves, twigs, and berries were brewed into teas or chewed fresh. The plant's warming nature helped to stimulate circulation, ease chills, and soothe the stomach. The berries, rich in essential oils, were used as a seasoning and medicinal spice. To those who lived close

WORKING WITH SPICEBUSH

Call on Spicebush when you are ready to awaken from a period of stillness, warm your spirit, and step forward with renewed energy. She helps clear away what lingers from the cold season, both in body and in heart.

If Spicebush grows in your area, take a quiet walk in the woods at dawn or dusk. When you find Spicebush, rest your hand on a branch and close your eyes. Listen. Ask a question and let her answer—through wind, birdsong, or sudden knowing.

"I am the secret breath of spring, slipping through the forest before the world has woken. Inhale my scent and remember something ancient . . . something waiting within you to rise."

The Spirit of Spicebush

to the land, Spicebush was both pantry and medicine chest, used fresh in the moment and also stored for leaner seasons. Her early blooms made her a seasonal marker, a symbol of hope in the weeks between winter and full spring.

Spicebush carries the energy of gentle awakening and protection. She is a herald of spring—a sign that light and warmth are returning. Her spirit encourages us to emerge from dormancy, rekindle our inner spark, and trust the steady renewal of life. Her aromatic presence also acts as a ward, clearing stagnant or unwelcome energies.

Hibiscus

Hibiscus species

With several hundred species, Hibiscus plants are well-known for their lush, luxurious, and outrageously eye-catching blossoms. Native to tropical and subtropical regions around the world, especially Asia, Africa, and the Pacific Islands, many varieties are cultivated for their vibrant blossoms, which range from deep crimson to delicate pinks and whites.

In traditional medicine, Hibiscus flowers, notably the red calyces (the outermost flower structure) of *H. sabdariffa*, have been used for centuries as refreshing, cooling infusions. In Ayurveda (an ancient holistic medicine system from India) and African herbalism, Hibiscus tea is valued for lowering body heat, supporting healthy blood pressure, lowering cholesterol levels, easing inflammation, and gently aiding digestion. Rich in antioxidants, it helps to nourish the heart and circulatory system.

"I am the blush of dawn and the song of summer. Open to me and I will show you how to bloom in your fullest color—fearless, radiant, and alive."

The Spirit of Hibiscus

Hibiscus embodies passion, beauty, and the flowering of the heart. She carries the energy of love in all its forms—self-love, romantic love, and universal compassion. Hibiscus encourages full self-expression, sensuality, and creative flow, reminding us to live vividly and openly. She is also linked to feminine energy, joy, and attraction, drawing sweetness and connection into life.

Across many cultures, Hibiscus is a symbol of welcome, hospitality, and lush beauty, and of honoring the preciousness of the present moment. In Hawaii, Hibiscus flowers are worn behind the ear to signal relationship status, while in other traditions this plant graces ceremonies, offerings, and celebrations of love.

WORKING WITH HIBISCUS

Call on Hibiscus when you wish to open your heart, awaken passion, or bring more vibrancy into your life. She is a reminder to savor the moment, to live fully in your beauty, and to allow your spirit to blossom.

Turn to Hibiscus for coolness under pressure, especially when things get "hot" and tempers flare. Experience her cooling energies through a tea meditation (see pages 57–61). Hibiscus makes a visually spectacular tea with rich shades of deep rose and reds. This can be brewed as a sun tea, with cold water and utilizing the Sun's energy, rather than steeping the tea in hot water.

Conclusion: Beyond the Veil

My dear friend, we have now come to my least favorite part of this journey—the ending. And yet, within every ending lives the seed of a new beginning. I truly hope this marks a beginning for you, one blessed by the Spirits of the Plants and this beautiful Earth.

This book has been written with you in mind. Yes, you. These words, ceremonies, meditations, and exercises have been shared to help you awaken to the world that exists beside our everyday reality. If you've taken even the first steps on this journey, then you've already begun to peer beyond the veil. There is so much more to life than what we perceive in this one realm. Infinite worlds exist just alongside our "ordinary reality," awaiting discovery, exploration, and celebration. As you read and reread these pages, and engage with the practices within, you'll walk your own sacred path with these remarkable beings.

It has been my profound joy to share this journey with you. Know that within every word of these pages is the immense love of the Plant Spirits, reaching out to inspire you, to guide you, and to gently call you home—home to your true self, and home to the Earth. If we are to continue living and thriving on this planet, we must learn to live in harmony with all beings. The Plant Spirits are sacred mediators in this process. They know the way. We need only follow.

Resources and Further Reading

Benyus, J. M. (2009) *Biomimicry: Innovation Inspired by Nature.* Mariner Books.

Darwin, C. (1880) *The Power of Movement in Plants.* John Murray.

Devi, L. (2008) *The Essential Flower Essence Handbook: For Perfect Well Being.* Crystal Clarity Publishers.

Gilbert, L. and Johnson, D. (2017) 'Chapter 4: Plant–Plant Communication Through Common Mycorrhizal Networks', *Advances in Botanical Research*, Vol. 82, pp. 83–97.

Hennessy, A. (2020) *The Healing Guide to Flower Essences: How to Use Gaia's Magick and Medicine for Wellness, Transformation, and Emotional Balance.* Fair Winds Press.

Kessler, A. *et al.* (2023) 'Volatile-mediated plant–plant communication and higher-level ecological dynamics', *Current Biology*, Vol. 33, Issue 11, pp. 519–29.

Khait, I. *et al.* (2023) 'Sounds emitted by plants under stress are airborne and informative', *Cell*, Vol. 186, Issue 7, pp. 1328–36.

Tompkins, P. and Bird, C. (1989) *The Secret Life of Plants: A Fascinating Account of the Physical, Emotional, and Spiritual Relations Between Plants and Man.* Harper & Row.

Whitehurst, T. (2013) *The Magic of Flowers: A Guide to their Metaphysical Uses & Properties.* Llewellyn.

Index

Acknowledgments

This book is dedicated to my dad who refused to carry me; my mom for always believing in me; Terry for her consistent love and kindness; Joe for his unwavering love and devotion; all my guides who have never left my side even in the darkest of times; MoonShadow, my constant writing companion; and the plants, without which we would not exist.

This book would not exist without the encouragement, trust, and dedication of so many beautiful beings along the way. To Carmel Edmonds and Kristine Pidkameny, thank you for seeing something in my work and inviting me into this journey. Your belief in this project gave it roots. To my editor, Imogen Valler-Miles, your thoughtful and meticulous guidance, care, and devotion to the voice of this book helped it bloom into its full expression. Thank you for walking beside me with such clarity and compassion. To my illustrator, Carolina Zambrano, your ability to bring the spirit of the plants to life through your art has added a sacred dimension to these pages. Your gift is felt in every line and leaf. Thank you for sharing your magic. To the Spirits of the Plants, you are the true authors of this work. I am merely the voice you chose to sing through. Your teachings have transformed my life, and I pray they continue to touch the hearts of many. To all of my teachers, human and otherwise, thank you for the wisdom you so generously shared. To my students—past and present—thank you for walking this green path with such openness, curiosity, and heart. You continue to inspire and remind me of why this work matters. And to the readers: may these pages open doorways, deepen your connection with the Earth, and remind you that you are never alone.